POPE PIUS XII LIBRARY, ST. JOSEPH COL.
3 2528 10582 5634

D1708143

design for fun: playgrounds

by Marta Rojals del Alamo

Editor: Carles Broto
Production: Jacobo Krauel
Author and Illustrator: Marta Rojals del Alamo
Translator: Amber Ockrassa
Texts for the projects were contributed by the designers

Cover photo: A. Legrain

Project concept: Carles Broto

Àusias March, 20. 08010 Barcelona, Spain
Tel.: +34 93 301 21 99 Fax: +34 93 30 00 21
www.linksbooks.net
info@linksbooks.net

Printed in Barcelona, Spain

design for fun:
playgrounds

Index

008 MAK
Plastic and Fantastic

014 Studio e.u
Italian Fragment

020 Bureau B+B
Waldpark

028 Kinnear Landscape Architects
Daubeney School

034 Chermayeff & Geismar
Kidpower

040 Environment Design Institute
Children's Plaza

046 Isabelle Devin & Catherine Rannou
Le Jardin des Insectes

050 Pasodoble (François Ghys & Ursula Kurz)
Le Dragon (La Villette)

056 Rehwaldt Landschaftsarchitekten
Wind-Wasser-Garten

062 Environment Design Institute
Asahikawa Shunkodai

068 Isabelle Devin & Catherine Rannou
Dunes

078 Knöll Okoplan
Trendsport Park

082 Bureau B+B
Looking for Jane

090 Sonic Architecture
PS 244

096 Knöll Okoplan
Vulkangarten

100 Heads Co., Ltd.
Akibadai Park

108 Art2architecture
Emslie Horniman

114 Cottrell & Vermeulen
Westborough Primary School

122 Andrés Nagel
Parc de l'Espanya Industrial

126 Chermayeff & Geismar
Urban Treehouse

130 Martirià Figueras
Hormigas

134 Taylor Cullity Lethlean & Mary Heavons
Hemmings Park

140 Sonic Architecture (Bill & Mary Buchen)
PS 23

146 Knöll Okoplan
Fliegergarten

150 Atsugi Kitawagara Architects Inc.
Fog Forest

154 Kinnear Landscape Architect
Helling Street Park

162 Greg Healey
Jimmy Melrose Park

164 Helle Nebelong
Valbyparken

176 Itsuko Hasegawa
Shonadai Cultural Center

184 Atelier de Launay
Parc de Sceaux

194 TAKANO Landscape Planning Co., Ltd.
Takino Suzuran Hill Park

204 Taylor Cullity Lethlean & Mary Heavons
Carlton Gardens Playground

212 Bureau B+B
Griendpark

216 Karin Zeitlhuber & Reinhard Bernsteiner
Die Welle

220 Büro Kiefer
Flämingstrasse

226 Kijo Rokkaku Architect & Associates
Shiru-ku Road

236 Bureau B+B
Valkenbergpark

238 Martirià Figueras
Reflejos

242 Robin Winogrond
Birken III

252 Bureau B+B
Beatrix Park

258 EMBT Arquitectes Associats SLP
The Magic Mountain

262 Knöll Okoplan
Pyramiden

266 Designing a Playground

Learning about the world through play

We tend to view the activity of playing as a non-serious pursuit -- kids' stuff -- with neither transcendence nor goal. We should remember, however, how much we ourselves learned during our earliest years while playing. Playing and learning are crucial for a child's development; and providing good play opportunities is a way to directly contribute to achieving this fundamental goal in the first stages of life.

From around the age of two onward, children spend more and more time playing, either alone or with adults at first and, later, with other children. Playing comes naturally; it forms part of children's daily activities and contributes to their physical, mental and emotional growth from the very start.

Not only do children release energy and develop motor skills, balance and coordination through play, but they also forge their personalities through social activities while stimulating creativity, the capacity to reason and language skills. Through play, children create custom-made realities and experiences. They learn to resolve problematic situations, confront new challenges and set their sights on new goals, all of which foments their capacity to organize, plan and make decisions. Play activities, therefore, are invaluable "dress rehearsals" for their future lives.

Plastic and Fantastic

Vienna, Austria

ron ARAD

mathilde BRÉTILLOT/ Frédérick VALETTE

andrée PUTMAN

denis SANTACHIARA

piotr SIERAKOWSKI

ettore SOTSASS

daniel WNUK

photographs: Hedjuk/MAK/Ziegler

©Hejduk/MAK

The exhibit "Plastic and Fantastic", presented in the MAK Gardens as a temporary experimental playground, focuses on building one's own world and experimenting with space, color, and material. The Vienna MAK was the exhibit's first stop outside of France before going on to a number of other European sites in view of a future collaboration between art, design and industry.

Conventional playgrounds leave children only little room to move, and the kids' possibilities of experience are quite restricted by the given structures and materials. This is why the French project group "*Les escarpolettes réinventées*" (The Reinvented Swings), under the direction of Martine Bedin, designer and co-founder of the Memphis Group, has invited an international team of designers, painters, and authors to create fantastic plastic objects. Children and grown-ups will be confronted with a new aesthetics of playing.

Renowned designers such as Ettore Sottsass, Andrée Putman, and Ron Arad, who had thus far dedicated themselves mainly to designing the "grown-ups' world", accepted the challenge and designed ten extraordinary plastic prototypes which are to be mass-produced. Plastic is the only material used; tight safety norms and spatial restrictions were the crucial components determining the design.

©Hejduk/MAK

Denis Santachiara designed this large creature, called "Big Pet, which with the help of an air pump looks like a huge, breathing animal.

©Hejduk/MAK

"Commence à construire!" (Start Building!): these huge colorful building blocks were contributed by the eminent architect and designer Ettore Sotsass.

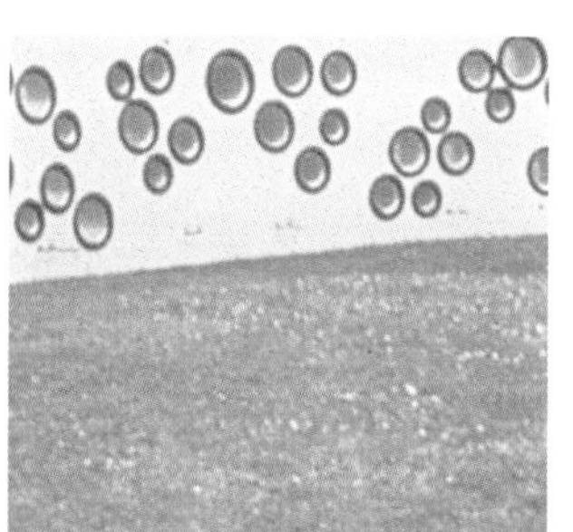
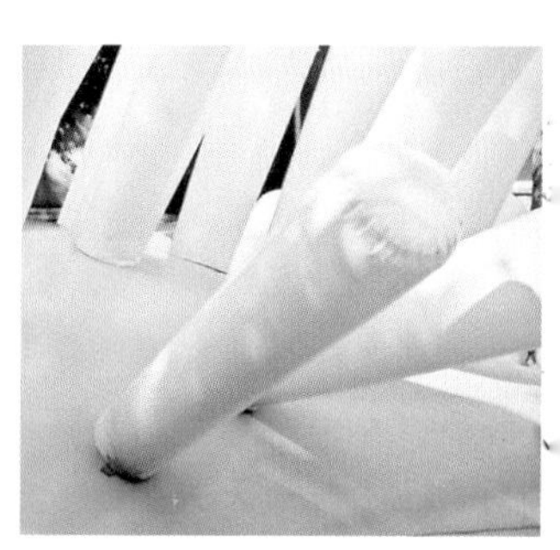

©Hejduk/MAK

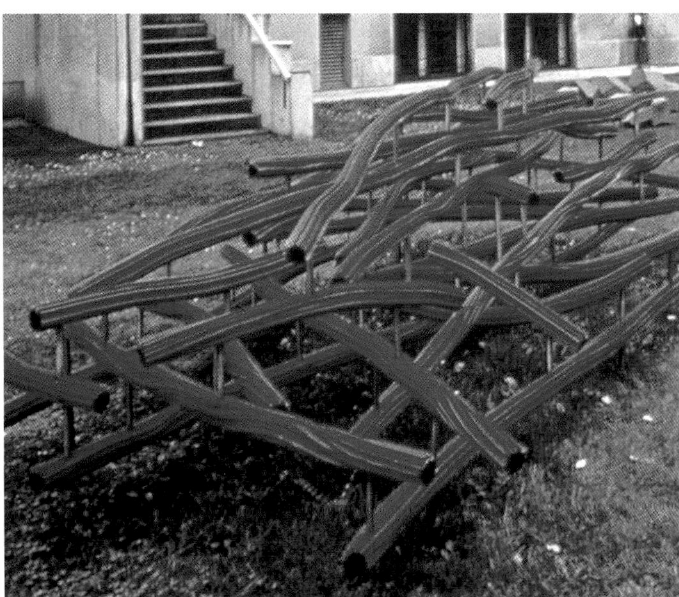

"*Siano*" is the name of this steel structure clad in fuchsia-colored foam and designed by Piotr Sierakowski. In the background, the stone labyrinth by Andrée Putman entitled "*Un jeu d'enfants*" ("Child's Play").

©Hejduk/MAK

The slide "*Hou Là Là*" was designed by Mathilde Brétillot and Frédérick Valette. "Memo Mountain" is by the prestigious designer Ron Arad.

©Ziegler/MAK

This wall, with its drums in varying sizes, has been given the onomatopoetic name of "Peng Pang Wall". It was created by Daniel Wnuk.

Italian Fragment

Grand-Métis, Quebec, Canada

Studio.eu

photographs contributed by the designers

What does it mean to say that a garden is "Italian", wondered the designers of this unique "fragment". What sort of relationship do Italians establish with nature? Italy enjoys a gorgeous historical landscape, "*il bel paese*", and the Italian people are known for their wholehearted desire to enjoy life. This desire to satisfy one's pleasures, to enjoy the "*bel paese*", however, often culminates in the act of altering it without respecting it. How can such concepts be represented in a garden?
Soccer and the soccer field comprise the theme garden *par excellence*. Indeed, with what do Italians occupy a great deal of their free time if not with a ball and the will to transform every beach and lawn into a soccer field? Yet, this wish to have playing fields scattered across the landscape, with the hundreds of gallons of water they require for their sustenance, is an issue that must be addressed in a country where water resources are thinning.
This garden for the festival of Méties is a symbolic fragment of Italy. A carpet-like lawn is gently raised to create a hill, on which one is invited to enjoy the sunset. At the same time, this topographic variation reveals the artifice that makes it possible: water. Visitors can extract it (contained in small bottles) and drink it.

italian fragment

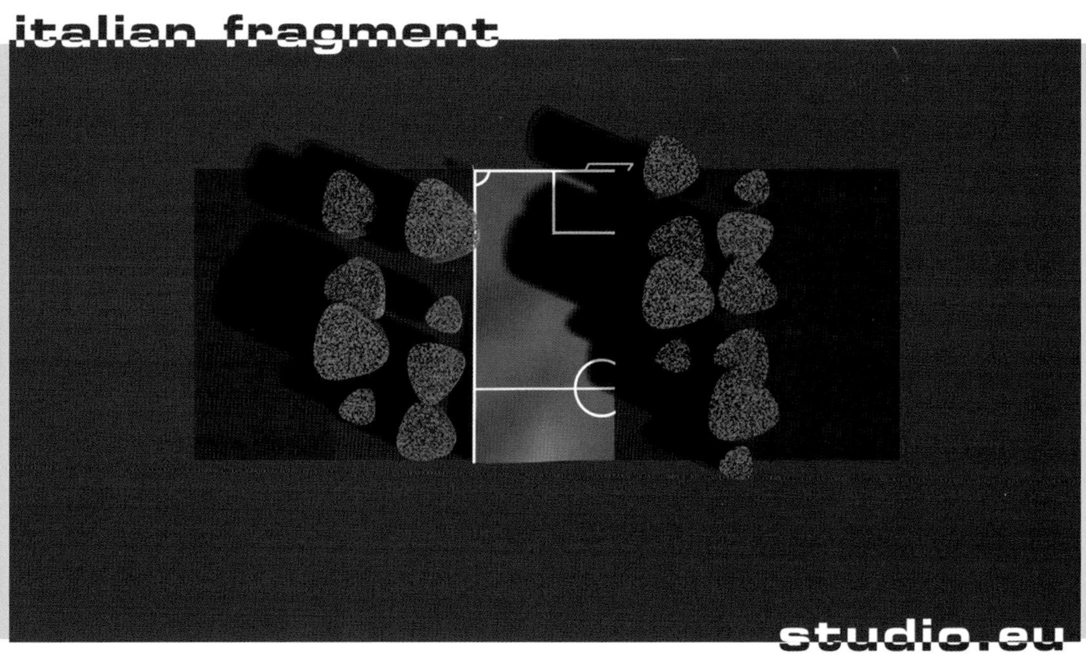

studio.eu

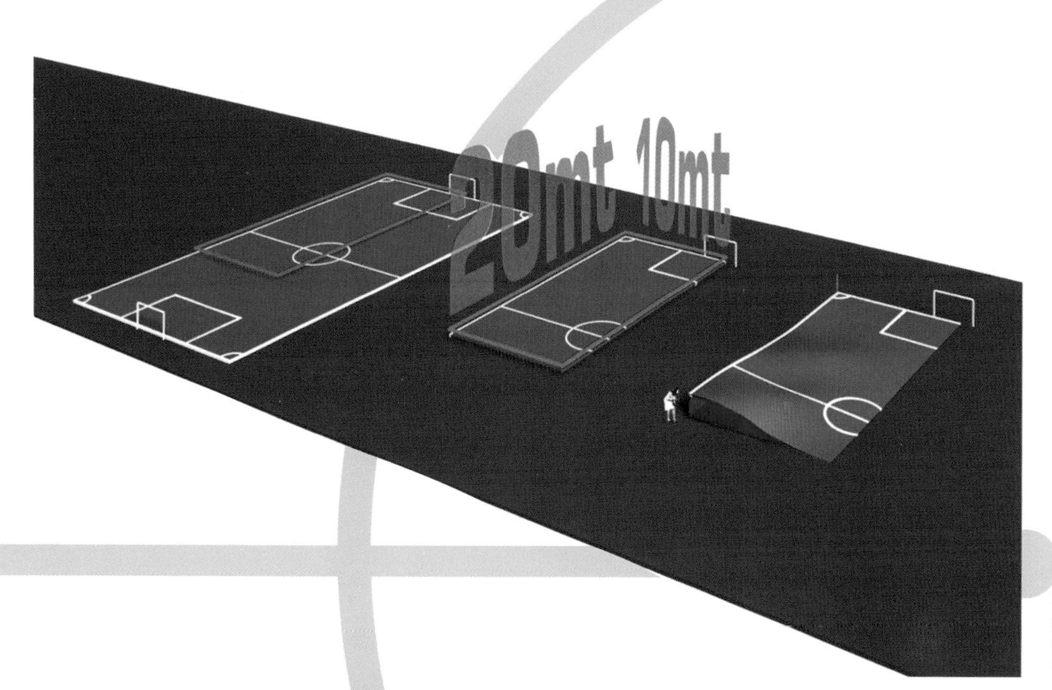

Bold white lines are a clear reference to the game of soccer, while the fragment of the goal posts is a frame for appreciating the surrounding landscape.

The wonderful Quebecois landscape is here transformed into soft, carpet-like grass, which is gently raised to create a hill.

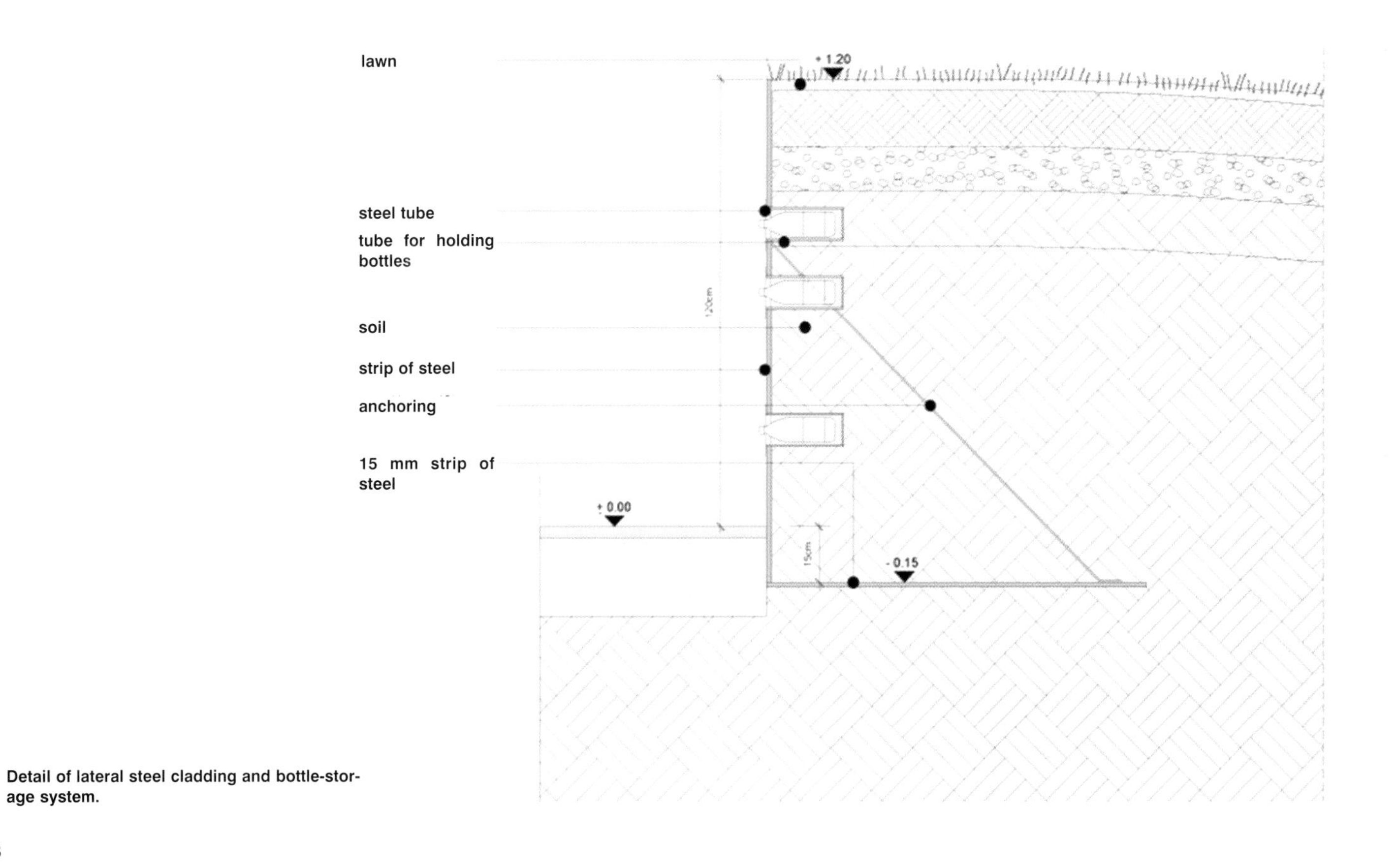

Detail of lateral steel cladding and bottle-storage system.

LA

Bureau B+B Photographs: Michael Lüder & B+B

Waldpark Potsdam

Potsdam, Germany

B+B won a competition to design a section of Bornstedter Feld, a former Russian military training camp that housed the central display of the national garden exhibit, Bundesgartenschau (BUGA), in 2001.
The goal was to create a dynamic recreational park with infrastructure for sports and games that would complement Potsdam's historical royal gardens, which continue to draw visitors both for their cultural aspects as well as for strolls through a natural setting. Thus, the idea of integrating a park into the existing natural environment and its ecosystem (a common goal in landscaping practices) was central to the design of Waldpark. The entirety of the budget went toward creating four large, eye-catching architectural objects cast in concrete. With their unique shapes and bold colors, these so-called "play terminals" draw visitors toward them and thereby become focal points for the park's most dynamic activities. Visitors take control of the objects, using them for all kinds of recreational ends, thereby drawing the main activity away from the more sensitive natural environment. BUGA's visit to Potsdam has thus enabled the consolidation of a unique, contemporary park in the city's natural and historic landscape - a park that also satisfies the recreational needs of a spectrum of visitors.

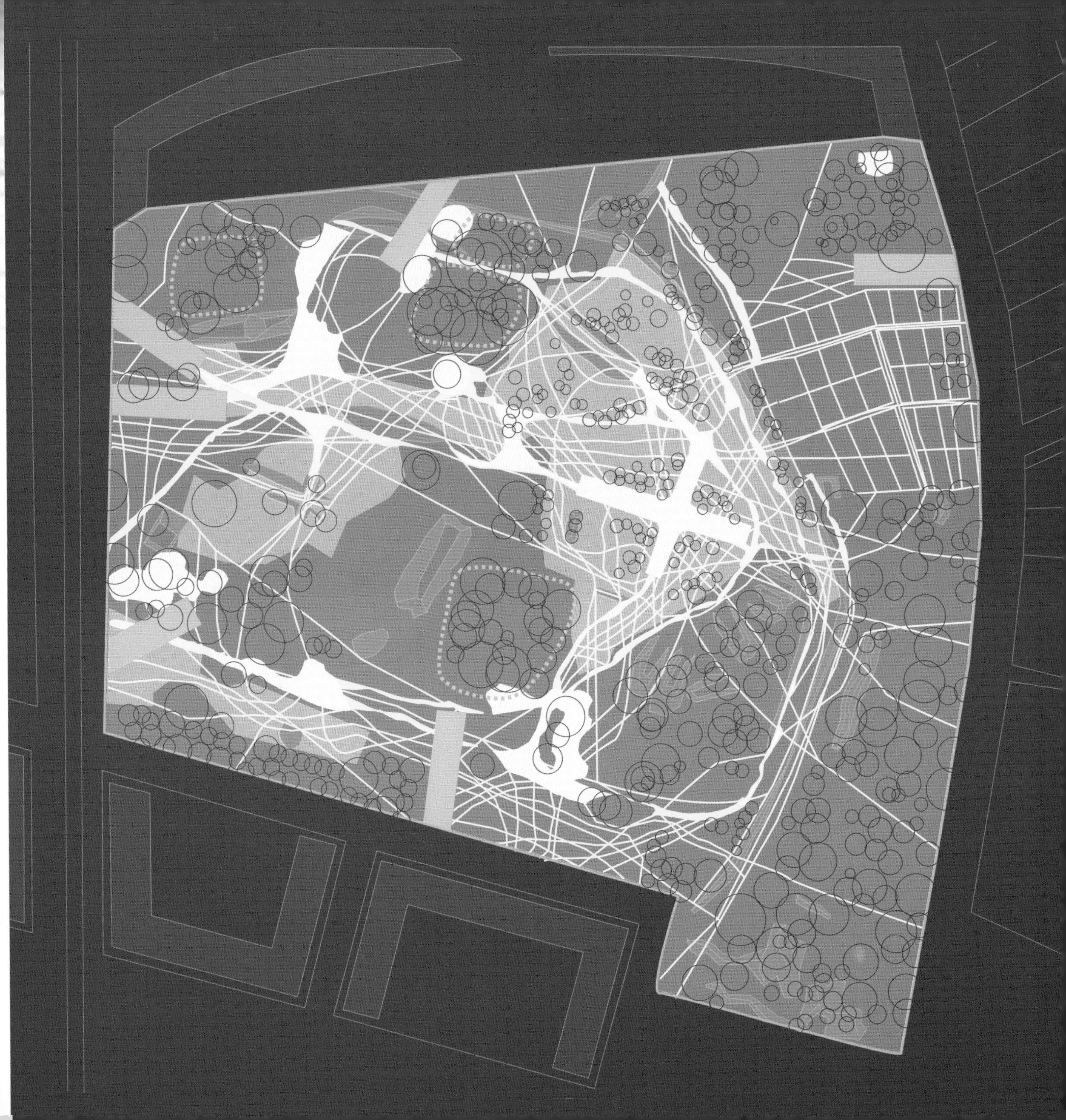

The play terminals, with their spectucular play equipment in pleasing colors and organic shapes, have been placed throughout the park at strategic points.

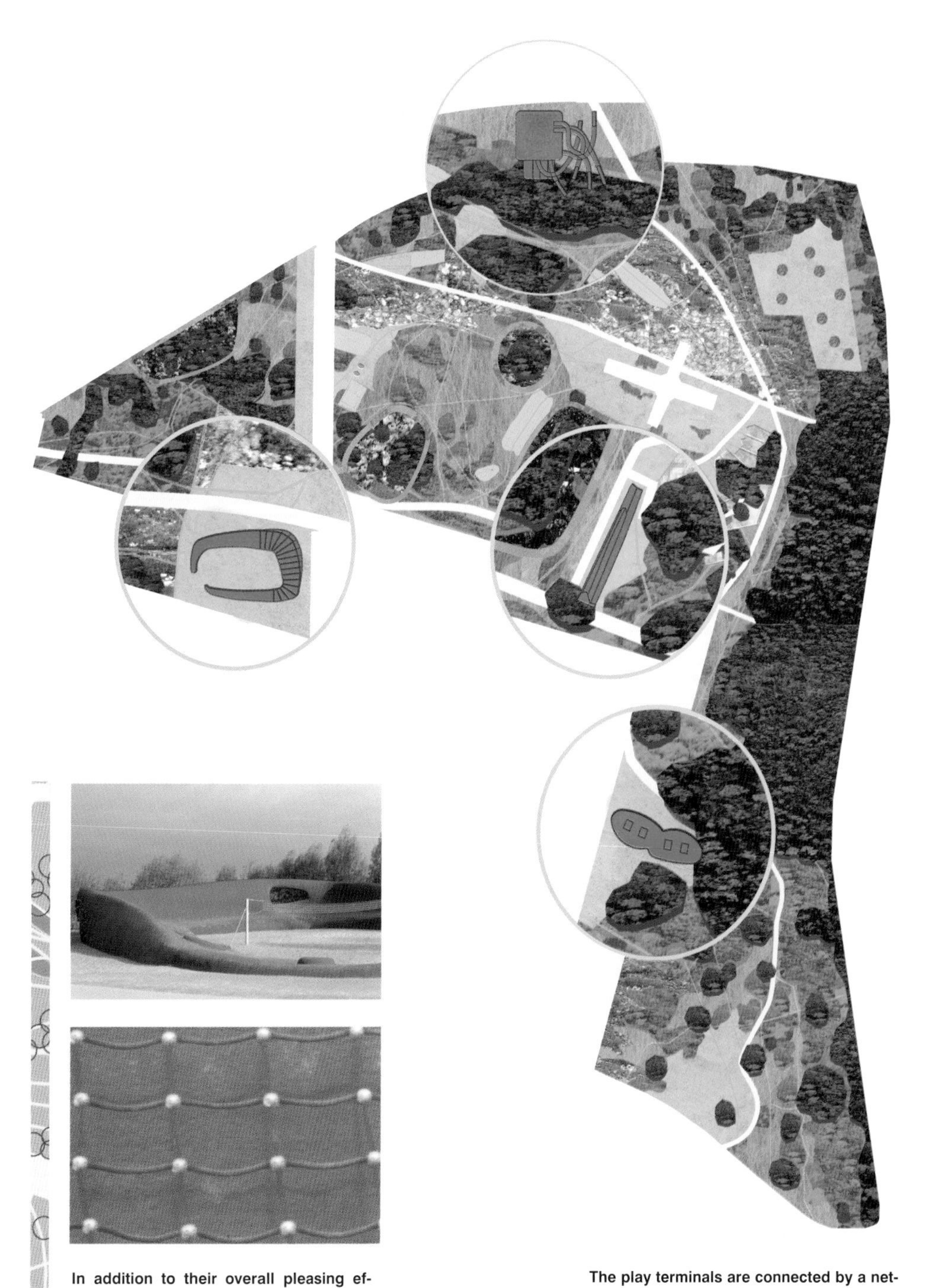

In addition to their overall pleasing effects, these structures include diverse elements for encouraging certain activities. Such elements include slides, trampolines and climbing nets.

The play terminals are connected by a network of narrow, semi-paved paths that meander through wild vegetation.

The rounded edges and smooth surfaces of these sculptures give them a soft, inviting aspect, in spite of the hardness of the material of which they are composed (concrete).

Who can resist the lure of this imposing fuscia sculpture beckoning to jump like a child on its elastic surface?

The plasticity of the terminals provides the perfect backdrop for theater performances or concerts; and their vertical surface lends itself nicely to slide projections, light shows and movies.

©Michael Lüder

In size, scale and color, these markedly artificial structures seem completely out of place; even so, they successfully interact with the natural surroundings precisely because they provide a contrast.

Daubeney School

London, UK

Kinnear Landscape Architects photographs contributed by the architects

Daubeney Primary School sits on a block of Victorian buildings in the center of London and has over 450 students ranging in age from three to eight years and hailing from a diversity of cultures. The design of this playground was presented as an alternative to the typical flat extension annexed onto an educational center where the primary activity is almost invariably soccer.
A very simple solution has produced maximum efficiency. This imaginative, constrast-filled design, based primarily on an expanse of asphalt with a low hill in the middle, encourages physical activity and interaction among the children through group games.
The ingredients (a "forest" of green posts, a dune which seems to reach beyond the bounds of the playground when reflected in a distorting mirror and white designs painted on black paving) visually divide and compartmentalize the area, thereby setting the stage for a variety of possible activities.

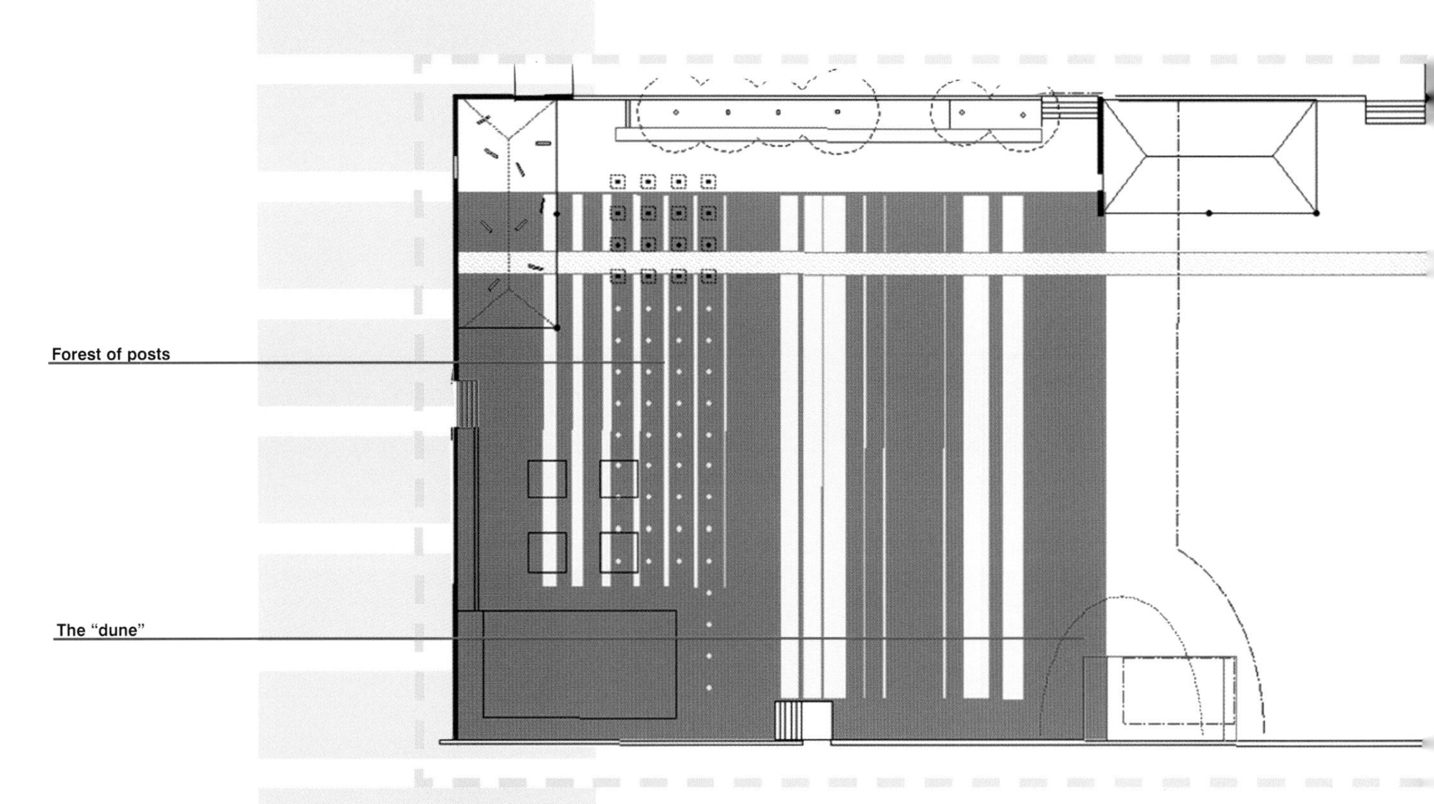

Ground plan of the playground

By incorporating these spectacular designs into the pavement, the ground surface is no longer a simple expanse of asphalt, becoming instead another element for encouraging play activities.

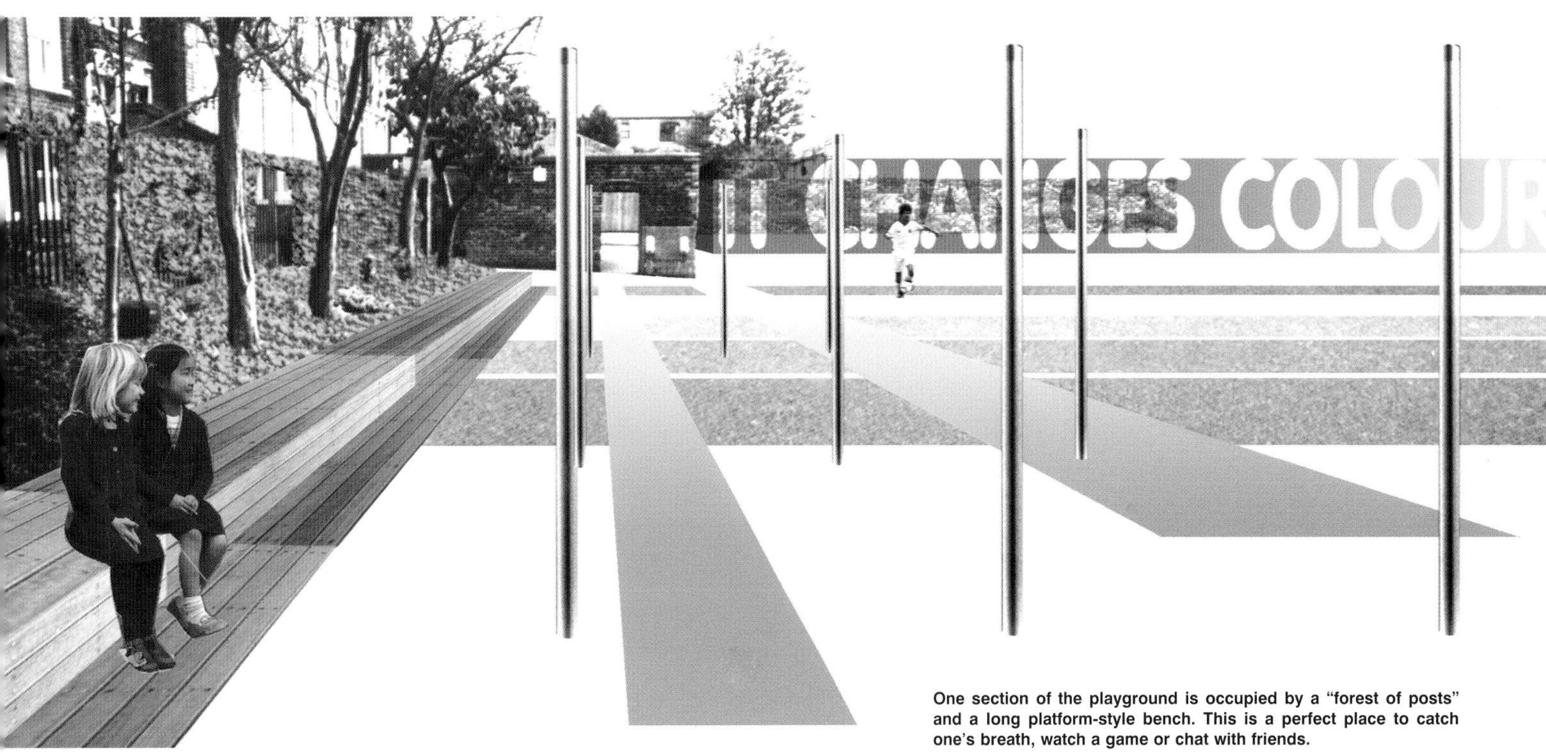

One section of the playground is occupied by a "forest of posts" and a long platform-style bench. This is a perfect place to catch one's breath, watch a game or chat with friends.

©Topos

Set against the backdrop of a reflective surface, the slope of a "dune" adds a sense of dynamism to an otherwise flat surface.

Boldly painted lines highlight the relief of the ground surface while encouraging the organization of all manner of alternative games and different types of activities.

Kidpower

New York City, USA

Chermayeff & Geismar

photographs contributed by the designers

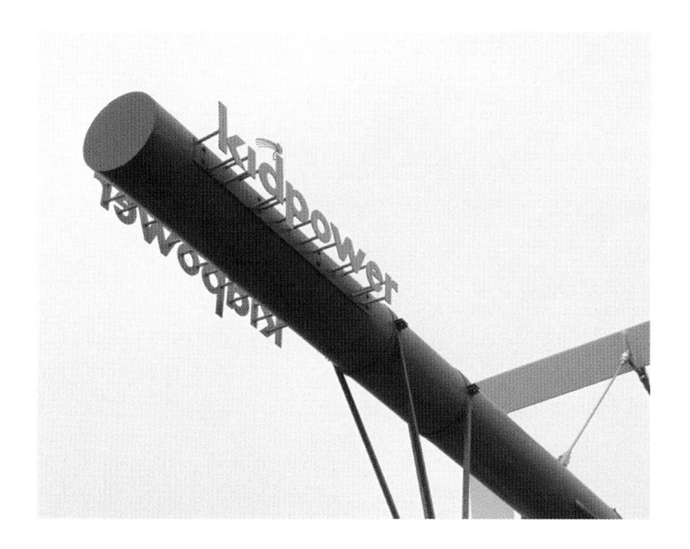

Comprising an important annex to the New York Hall of Science, this 30,000-square-foot outdoor children's playground features dozens of fun activities, each of which is geared toward teaching a scientific principle. Here, everything that involves children presents an opportunity to experience and learn something about physics, sound and the value of shared, communal involvement.

When compared to an indoor science exhibit or a classroom science lecture, this space is far more effective and didactic, as it actively engages children's interest. Here, one finds a parabola that reflects sound; there, kids are introduced to the basics of physics on slides and teeter-totters. Without even realizing it, children learn valuable lessons here about the world around them; and they do so while thoroughly enjoying themselves!

"The western hemisphere's largest science playground" is entertaining for all age groups.

A "whisper dish" collects and amplifies even the most distant or quiet sounds.

Here, kids get hands-on learning about hydrodynamics, without even realizing they're receiving a science lesson!

This massive web-like structure teaches the concept that “for every action there is a reaction”.

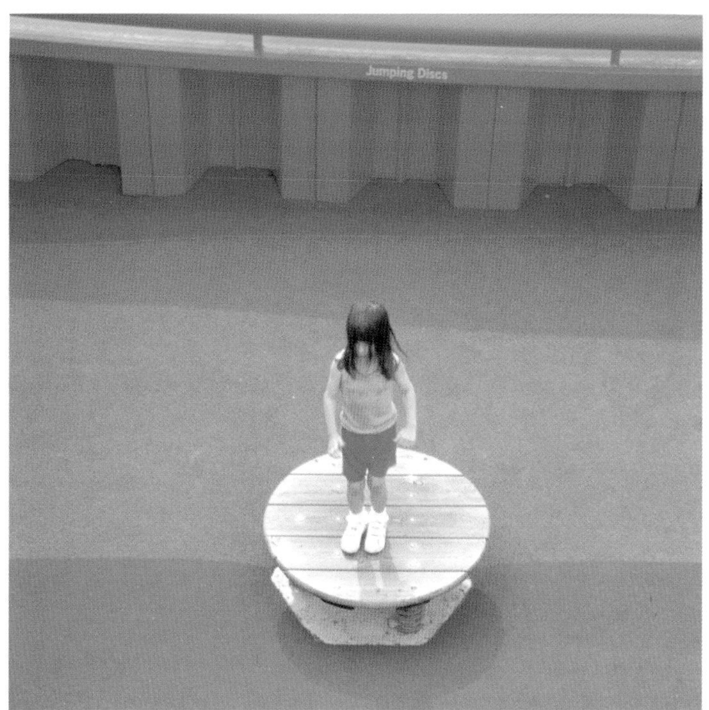
Jumping Discs

Children's Plaza

Tsukuba City, Japan

Environment Design Institute

photographs contributed by the designers

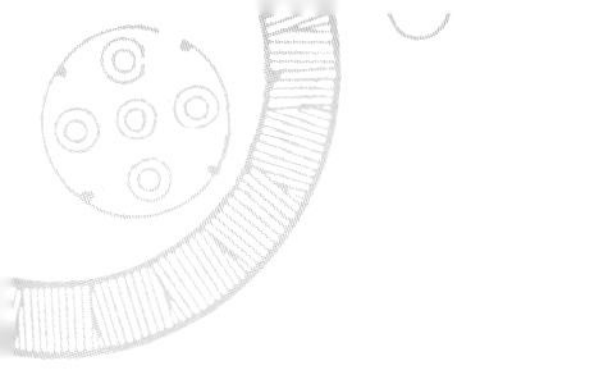

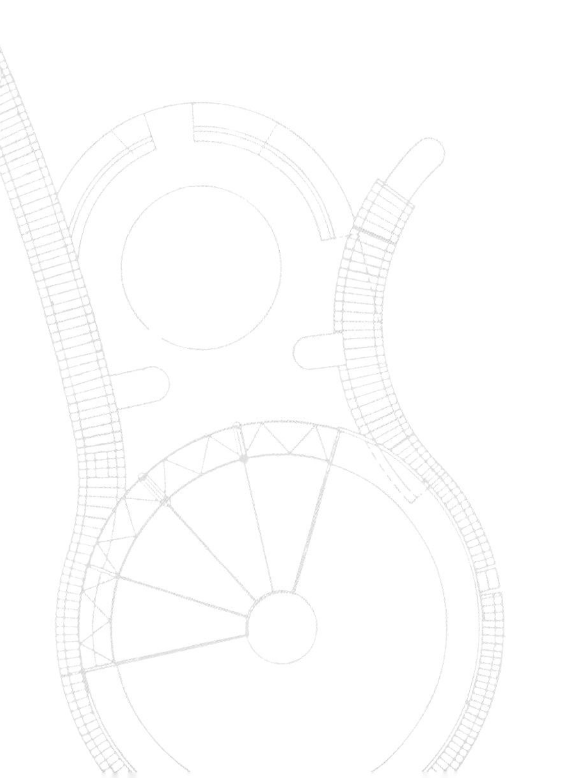

This children's plaza, a facility exhibited at the Tsukuba Science Expo, is situated at the center of the Expo site. It is divided into four themes. The first is the "Garden of Wonder", which features numerous optical illusions to delight children of all ages. The second is a "Fun Tube", which is a 270-meter-long, 2.7-meter-diameter tube structure serving as a science exploratorium. The third is a "Mechanimal", and the fourth is the "Japanese Archipelago Zone", which re-creates a sector of the globe at a scale of 1/100,000, and measures 36 meters in width.

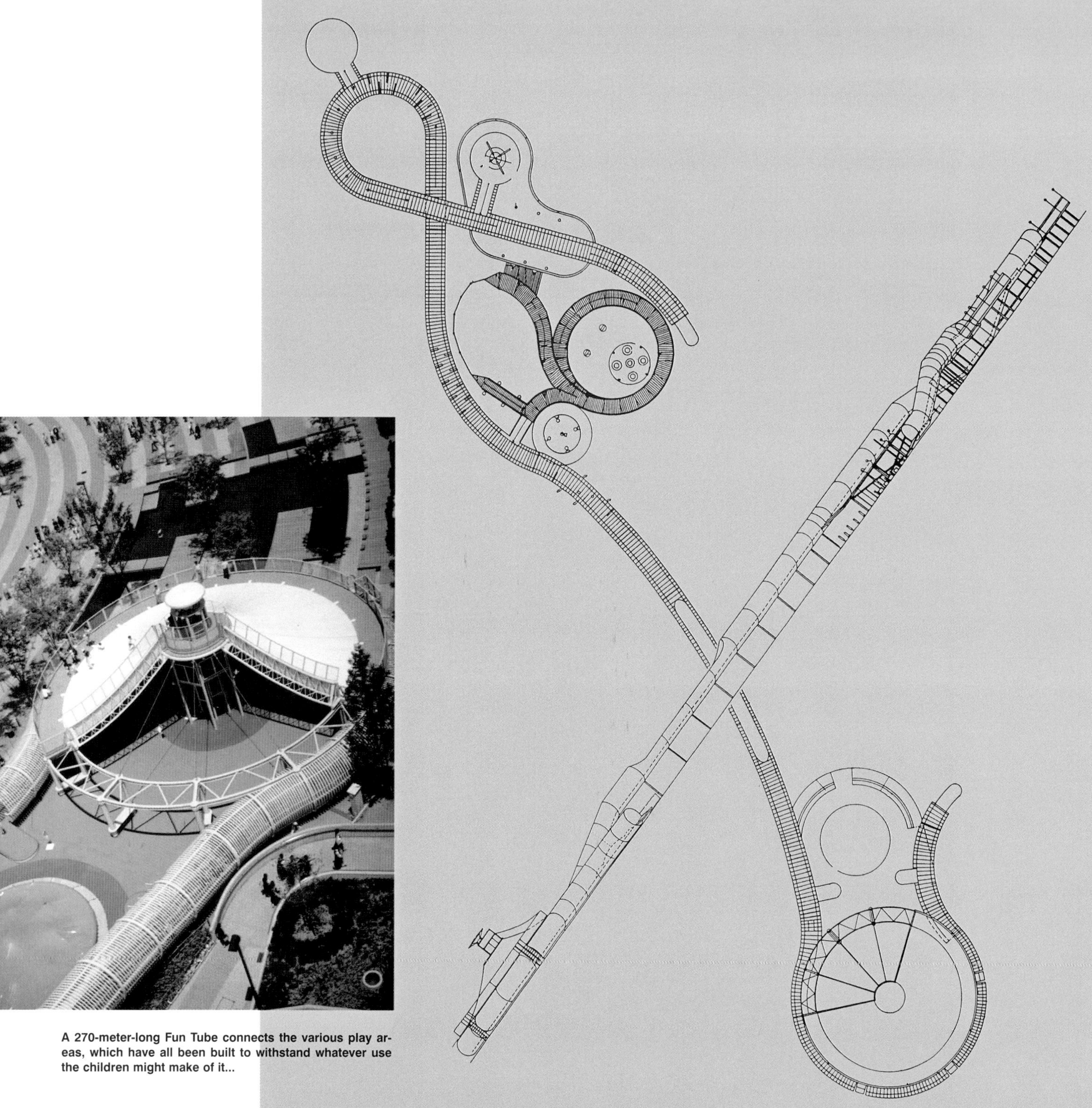

A 270-meter-long Fun Tube connects the various play areas, which have all been built to withstand whatever use the children might make of it...

...For example, the roof provides shade and is also a massive slide.

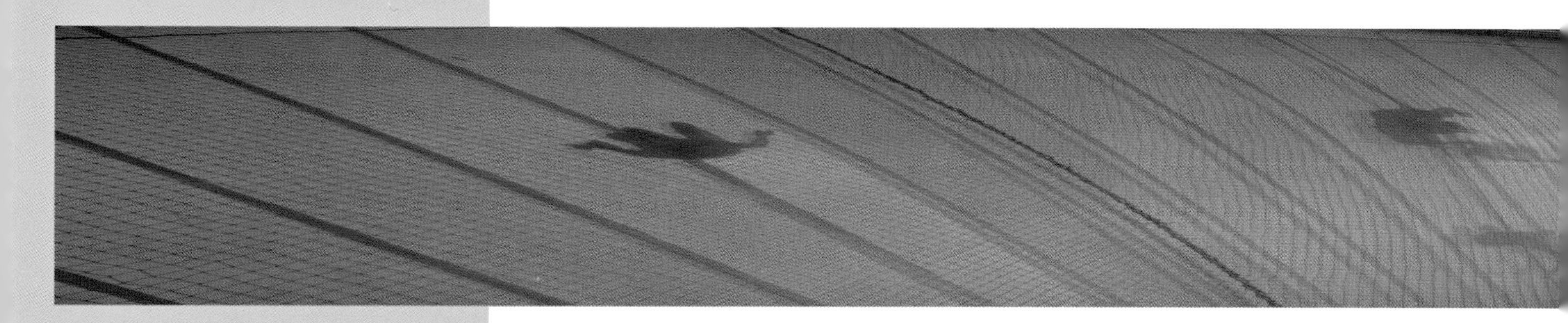

The spaces successfully combine aspects which are at once aesthetically pleasing and educational. Here, views of the Fun Tube, the Garden of Wonder and the Japanese Archipelago, which is slightly curved to give the idea of its place on the globe.

Le Jardin des Insectes

Paris, France

Isabelle Devin & Catherine Rannou photographs: A. Gui

The Insect Garden is located in a strip of the Boulogne Forest in the heart of the Acclimation Garden, and contributes to the restructuring of this historic park.
The playground, which is intended for children between the ages of 6 and 12, occupies a sandy plot hemmed in by a band of trees and shrubs. The children, therefore, play in an environment that changes and evolves with the seasonal cycle. The rapid annual growth of the plant species chosen means that the space is "cleaned out" in the winter, when the leaves have all fallen, while in the summer, when most of the vegetation is well over two meters tall, the area is densely enclosed.
Beyond this vegetated boundary, the playground equipment with its most eye-catching elements can be appreciated: teeter-totters from which sprout long curved bars with insects clinging to the ends.

A dense layer of trees and shrubbery hides the park in the summer, when it reaches a height of over two meters.

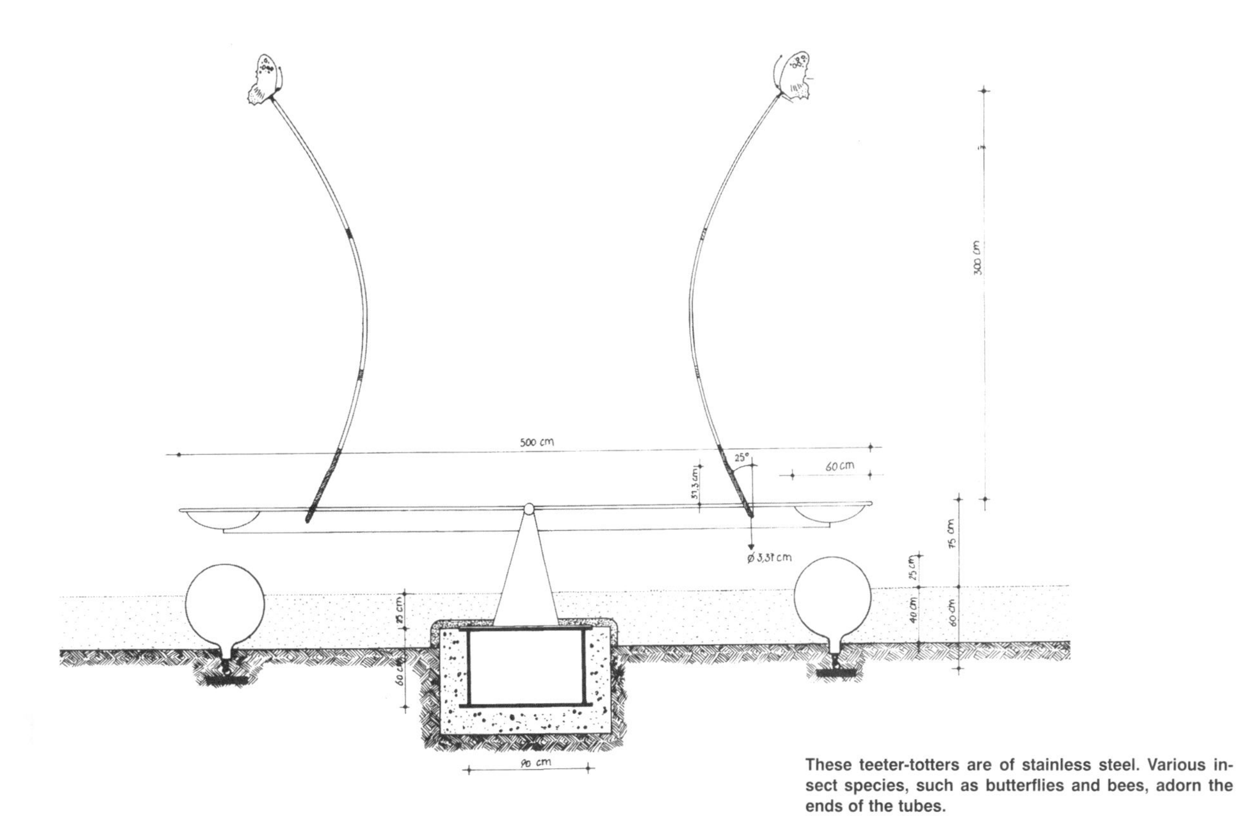

These teeter-totters are of stainless steel. Various insect species, such as butterflies and bees, adorn the ends of the tubes.

PasoDoble

Françaois ghys & Ursula Kutrz

photographs contributed by the architects

Le Dragon Parc de la Villette Paris, France

Created in the 1970s, even before the Parc de la Villette saw the light of day, the mythical Villette Dragon has now been renovated. The project was carried out by its designer, François Ghys, in order to move it to the theme park specifically designed by Ursula Kurz, who was working at the time of the project with the Bernhard Tschumi team.
The dragon was brought into line with European safety norms and the legs that we now see were added as a substitute for the original support network which was deemed unsafe. By attaching bristly appendages, it acquires the look of an authentic dragon that may just disappear at any moment. Only the new stairs and the slide on one side, along with the ropes thrown over it like a giant Gulliver-Dragon, seem to hold it in place. Composed of circular sections of wood in varying sizes, the body of the dragon curves across its allotted ground space and crosses through the different sequences of the garden, showing off its impressive size.

Children play hide-and-seek inside the body, while the bigger kids climb up the back to reach the huge stainless steel tongue-slide.

The formidable image of this mythological figure is glimpsed intermittently between the leaves of the vegetation, thereby accenting its monumental nature.

Having overcome the initial fear of the height, small and big kids alike quickly and impatiently scramble to climb back up again.

Wind-Wasser-Garten

Leipzig, Germany

Rehwaldt Landschaftsarchitekten

photographs: **Rehwaldt Landschaftarchitekten**

Nobody would suspect that this colorful fish pond sits on land (located south of Leipzig) that was once used extensively for mineral mining and whose highly toxic effects proved devastating for the area's natural, cultural and historical landscape. With the end of mining practices here came new possibilities for the region: the water from the subsoil was regenerated and Lake Cospuden emerged as a new recreation area near the center of the city. Various water parks have been constructed along an axis measuring several miles in length, linking the urbanized terrain to Cospuden. Each park uses water or the idea of water in its composition. The Wind-Water Garden is a pond in its own right and has been built so that when the water from the subsoil rises, its basin is filled as if it were a dam. Set near the "Lauer Waldteich" lake, it is a whimsical interpretation of this special place in which water is a central theme.

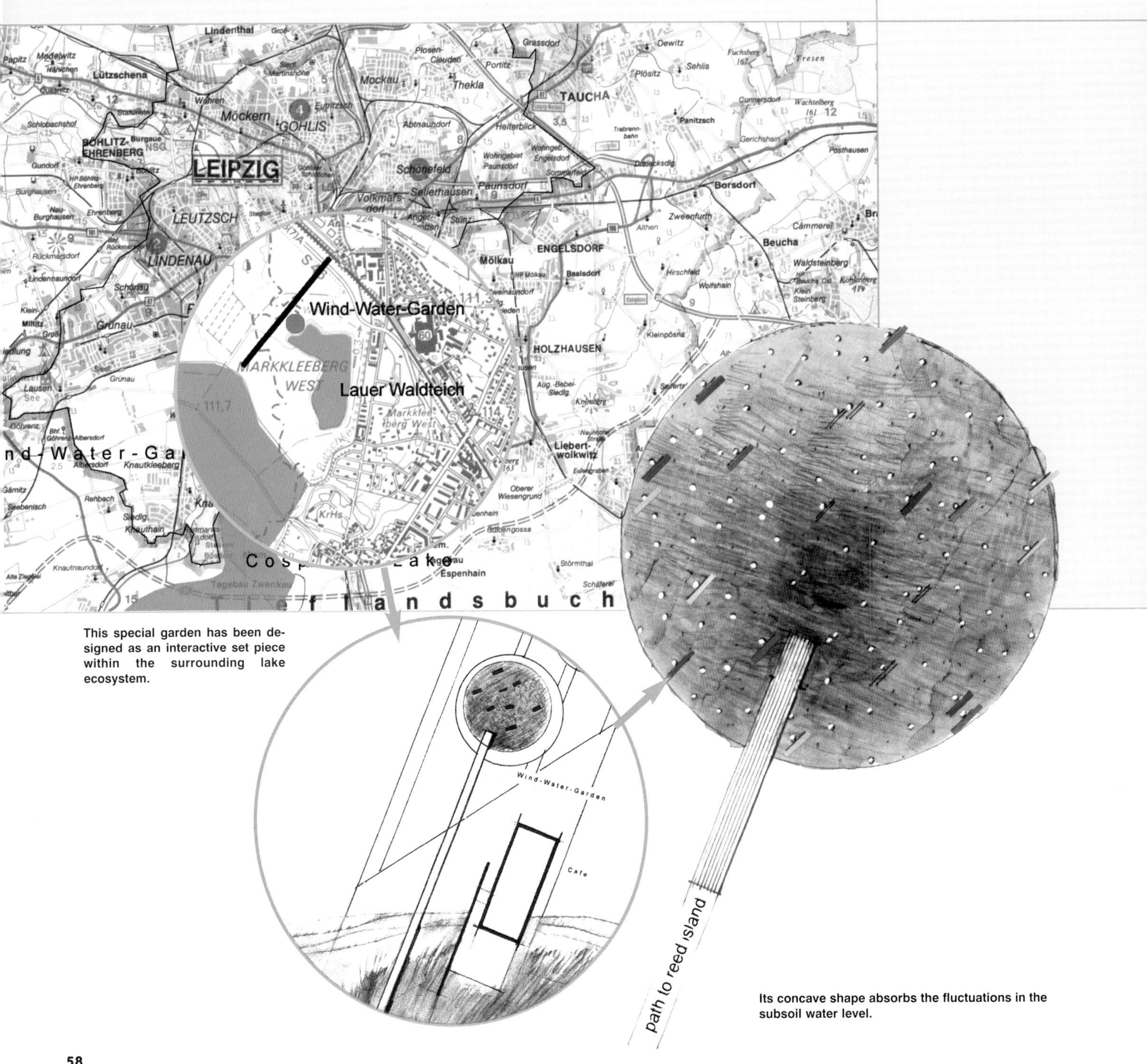

This special garden has been designed as an interactive set piece within the surrounding lake ecosystem.

Its concave shape absorbs the fluctuations in the subsoil water level.

Grass covers the bottom of the bowl like a soft green carpet and a narrow, curving path leads to the bottom.

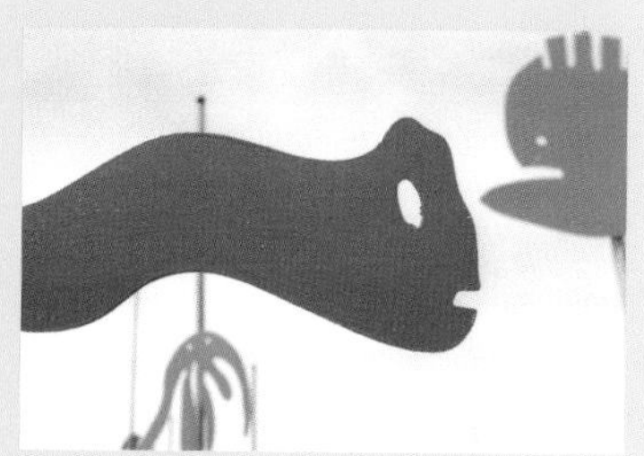

The long steel posts are a stylized interpretation of the reeds which so often grace watery environments.

This allusion is reinforced by the inclusion of natural reeds, which sway in the wind along with the colorful figures of aquatic animals attached to posts.

Like flags blowing in the breeze, they create an attractive plastic effect that is multiplied by reflections whenever the water rises.

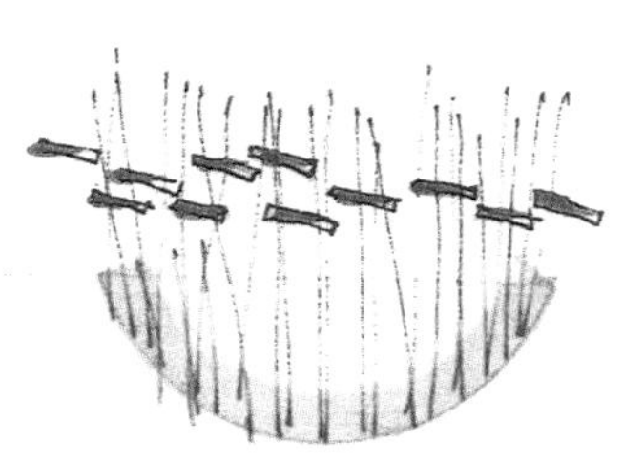

reeds and water animals

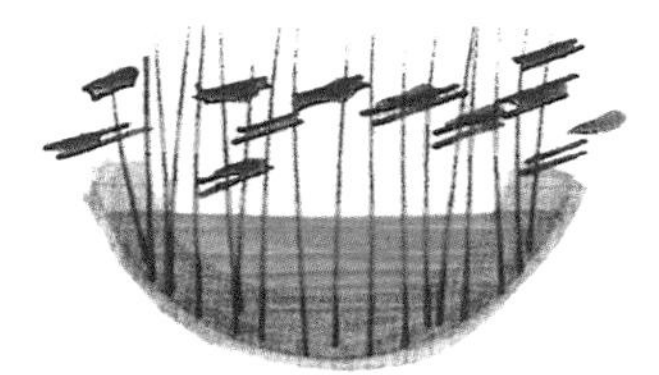

reeds, water animals and water

Subsoil water flow is a dynamic system and variations in its level can be observed in the park.

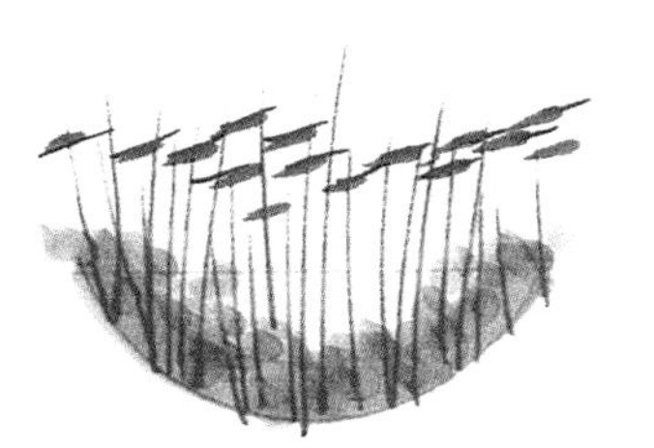

Spring - caltha palustris.

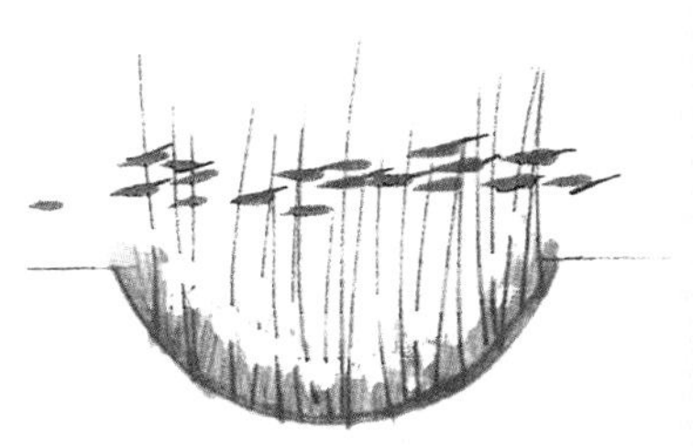

Autumn - Filipendula ulmaria.

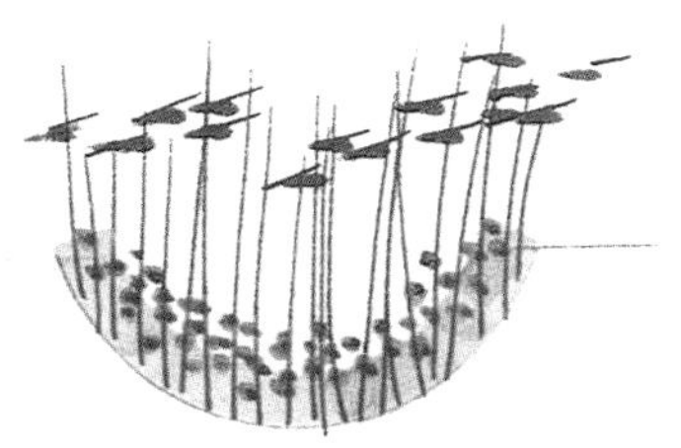

Summer - geranium pratense.

winter - frozen lake

The cycle of the seasons is also reflected in the garden's plant species.

Asahikawa Shunkodai Park

Hokkaido, Japan

Environment Design Institute photographs contributed by the designers

This massive structure, enjoying 485 m^2 of floor area, is the first two-story roofed playground in Japan. It is located in the new residential development of Shunkodai in Asahikawa and was developed as a play structure with a large roof to make it usable as late as possible in the season in an area known for its heavy winter snowfall. It was built primarily in wood (for warmth and style) and steel (for durability).

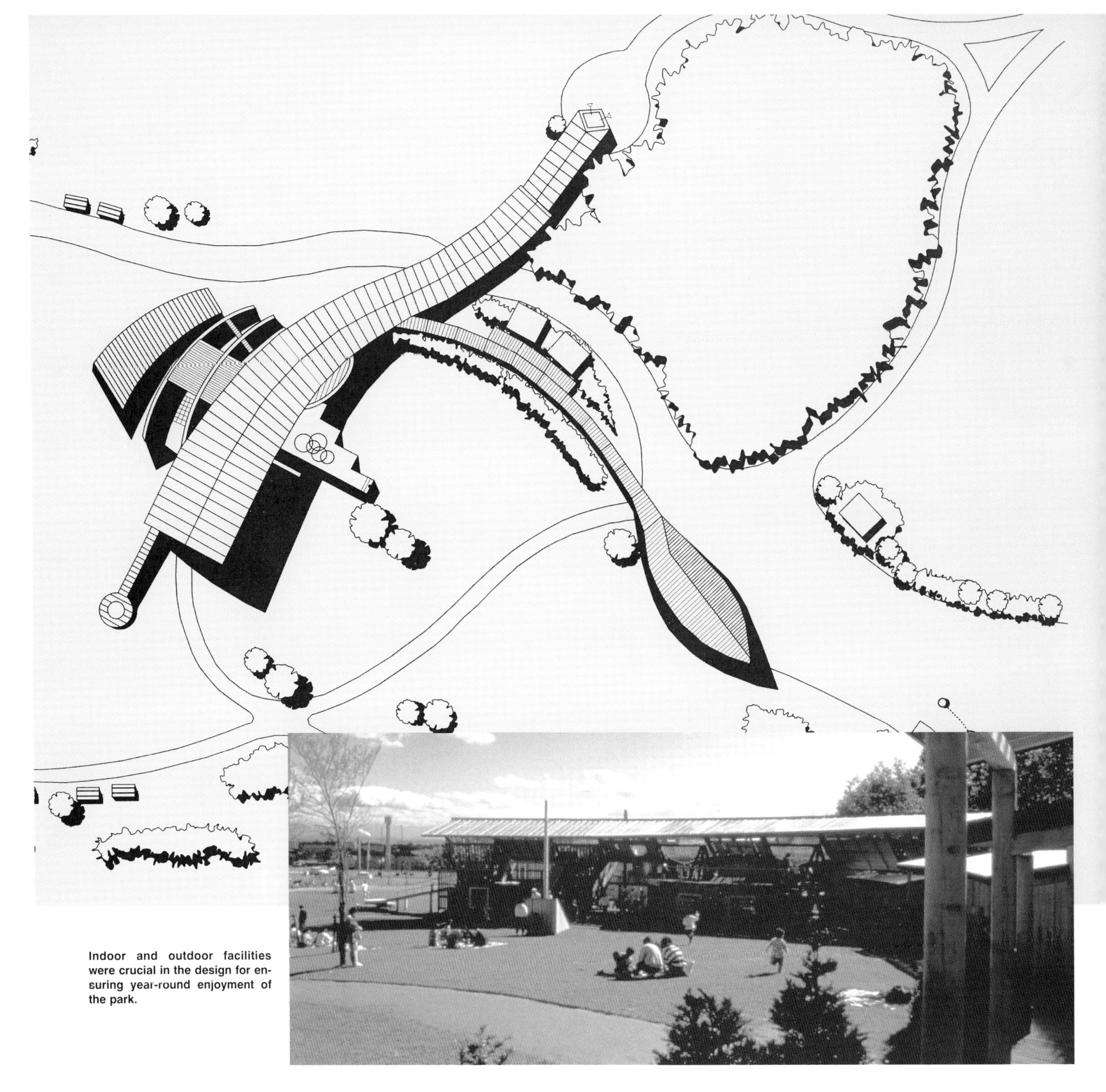

Indoor and outdoor facilities were crucial in the design for ensuring year-round enjoyment of the park.

Even when playing indoors in the winter months, children are given as ample views as possible of the outdoors.

The designers wished to make a space that would be at once aesthetically pleasing and fun, using a mixture of materials that would give it both a modern look and a cozy feel.

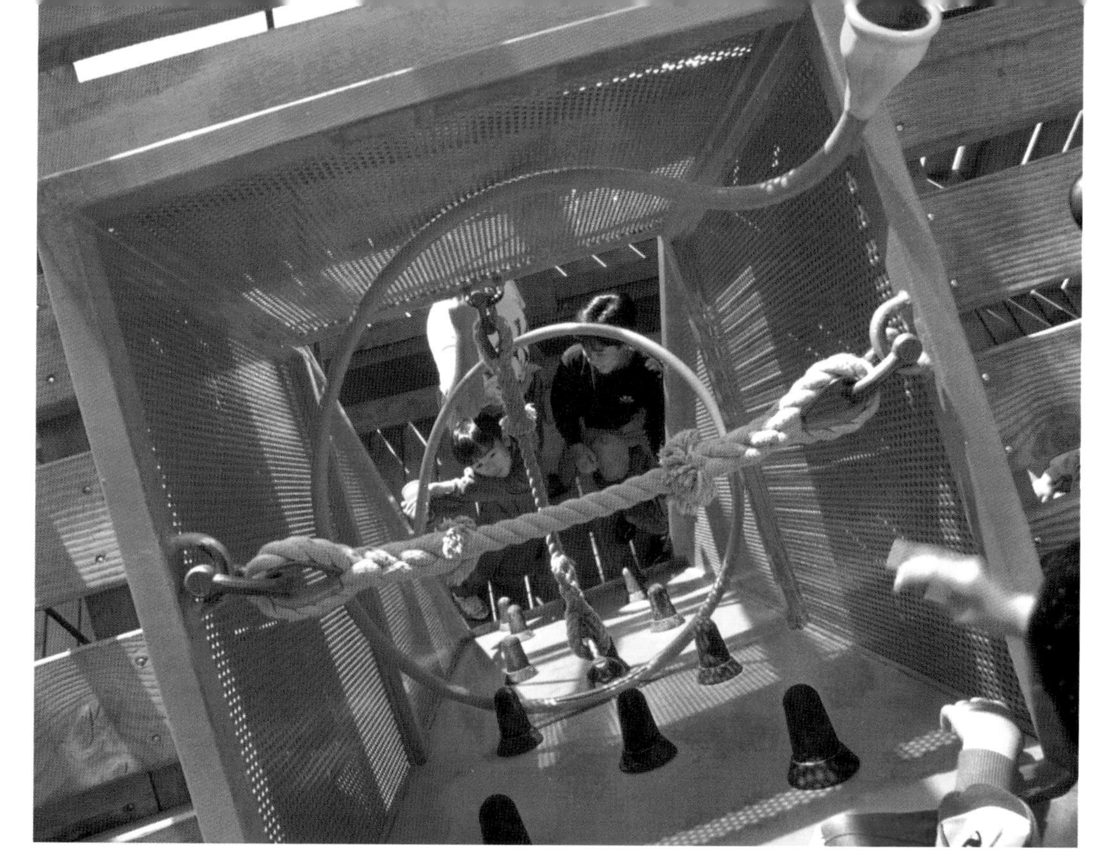

Elements with varying degrees of difficulty were included to stimulate and challenge kids of all ages.

More than a simple design feature, these ingenious hollow tubes have a mouthpiece at each end for communicating at both ends of the climbing tower.

Jardin des Dunes

Paris, France

Isabelle Devin & Catherine Rannou

photographs: H.Abbadie; A. Goustard; X. Testelin; S. Reggiardo; A. Legrain

©A. Legrain

©X. Testelin

©A. Legrain

This "Dune Park", which is located in the heart of Villette park on the banks of the Ourcq canal, has been designed as a prototype. Based on the concept of creating a landscape which in and of itself would be entertaining, a single space becomes both the stage for and generator of games, creating a tight-knit relationship with the children in the form of a dialogue between their movement and the landscape.
A seascape has been created in the park, brought about through the treatment of the details as well as in the selection of material and the themes for the games. The gentle rise and fall of the land, the materials, plants, atmospheric elements and the visual and auditory stimuli all come together to form this stage set, creating an overall atmosphere that brings about a sense of wellbeing.
Some of the playground equipment has been custom-designed for this project. Many pieces are repeated throughout the park, allowing the greatest number of children to play at the same time without creating friction or frustration, while encouraging social involvement in a fun setting.

©H. Abbadie

An implicit sense of movement in the playground can be appreciated in the original model; boredom here is out of the question.

©H. Abbadie

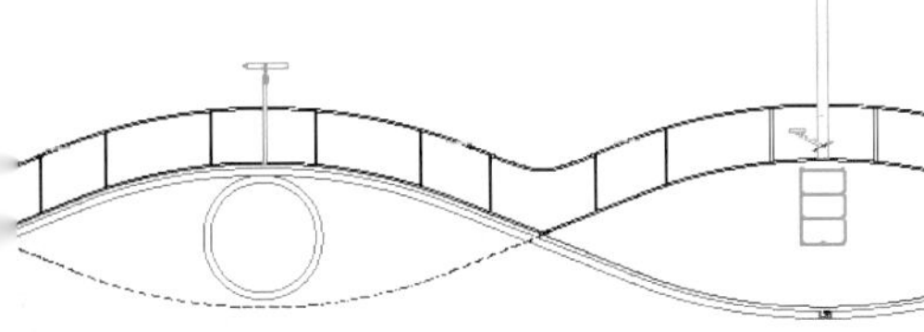

The playground equipment is scattered throughout the "seascape" of the playground, many pieces being repeated so that as many children as possible can play on them at the same time.

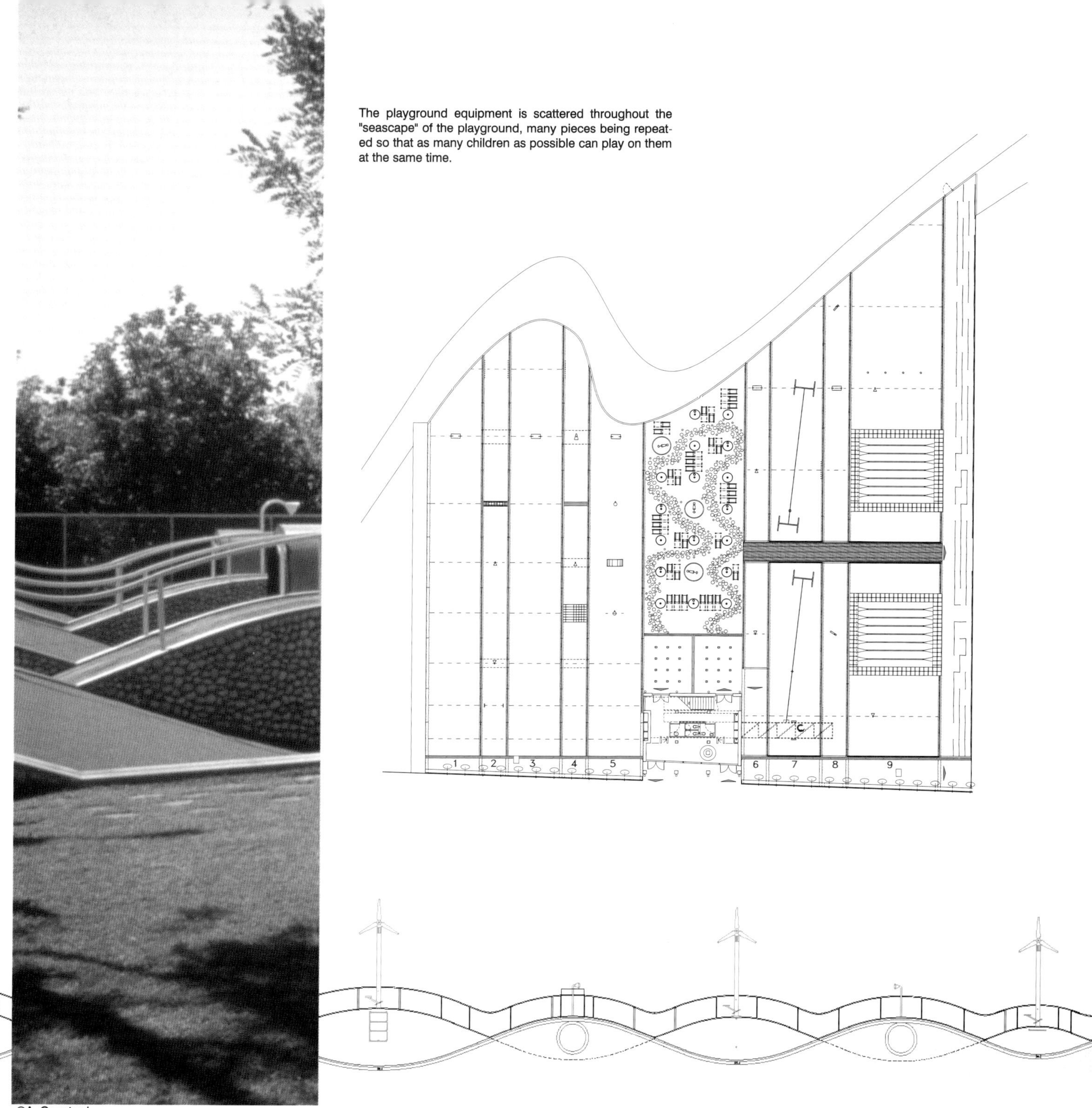

©A. Goustard

©A. Legrain

Few can resist the temptation to test their strength against that of the wind with these "wind pedals".

Kids can run to their heart's content inside this giant "hamster's wheel".

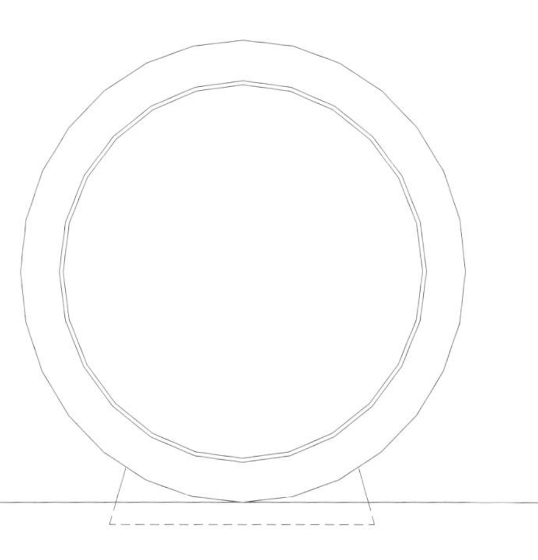

©A. Legrain

Children love this huge air mattress, and prove it by running and jumping non-stop over its springy surface.

©X. Testelin

Acoustic phenomena have also been worked into the park in the form of whimsical megaphones.

Bernard Tschumi's famous "follies" serve as spatial markers that fill the space with color.

The park is brimming with elements, such as this bridge-net, that encourage physical activity.

©S. Reggiardo

©X.Testelin

The rise and fall of the hills creates a landscape of great plastic beauty that alternately conceals and reveals the various areas for playing and relaxing.

Trendsport

Ostfildern, Germany

KNÖLL OKOPLAN photographs: **Andreas Peyker**

At the start of the planning process, a program was discussed that took into account the combined input of designers, planning experts, local youth groups and city administration employees. Through this process, the sports that were to be included in the "Trendsport Park" were decided upon: skating, in-line hockey, climbing, volleyball and street-ball.
Zoning regulations stipulated that the planes intended for the various sports should be easily identified as horizontal surfaces. However, some sports require inclined or vertical surfaces. As a result, the climbing walls and halfpipes were not set up in high places, but rather in the most sunken points of the site. Thus, the park takes on the aspect of the landscape's negative, with spaces carved out of flat planes and then "filled" with sporting installations. A wide expanse of asphalt links the various zones.
Trendsport Park has given the neighborhood a completely open sporting installation, freely accessible with no entrance fees nor membership cards. A youth center is being planned which will sit adjacent to the park at the same height as the parking lot.

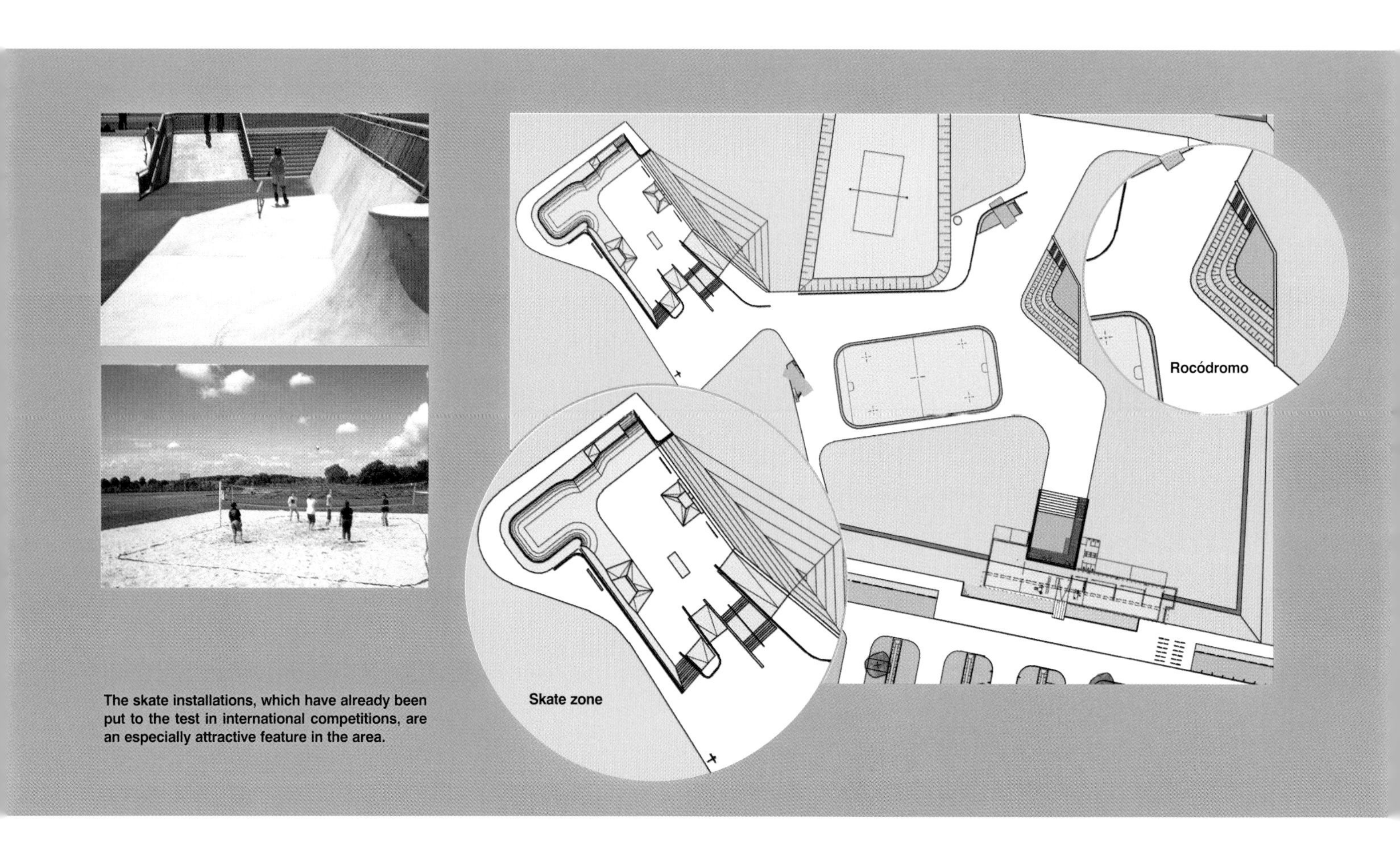

The skate installations, which have already been put to the test in international competitions, are an especially attractive feature in the area.

This climbing wall, which has been built into a retaining wall, was made possible by the features of the terrain.

Skaters and rollerbladers cover changes in level of two meters via ramps and stairs, with various obstacles along the way. The entire installation was built, and the concrete poured and clad, *in situ*.

Every last element within the bounds of this area can be put to use by the skaters and rollerbladers who come here.

Bureau B+B Photographs: Matthijs Hens & B+B

Garden no. 16

"Looking for Jane"

Houten, Holland

While the term "garden" generally conjures the image of an enclosed parcel of landscaped terrain set amidst rural surroundings, that concept has been turned on its head in this park. "Looking for Jane" is a wild, untended place that has been fenced in and surrounded by a garden, the Makeblijde, which is a site formerly occupied by a school.

The mysterious atmosphere of a wild garden was part of the design from the start, making "Looking for Jane" an enchanting place which visitors feel inspired to explore. From a distance, a rough wooden fence takes on the appearance of a large black box emerging from the middle of an orchard.

In searching for the entrance, visitors are guided around the garden until coming upon a movable section that swings open to allow passage. Once inside, visitors are immersed in a jungle of wild vegetation (this is the former school's garden with the addition of exotic plants) where there are no paths and where the only paving consists of a thin layer of bark chips. The high fence and the mist rising from the existing stream come together to create an ideal microclimate for the exotic plants, thereby heightening the illusion of wandering through a jungle.

Visitors do a balancing act across fallen trunks or use a narrow bridge to reach the far side of the jungle, where the fence encloses a dark, enchanted space.

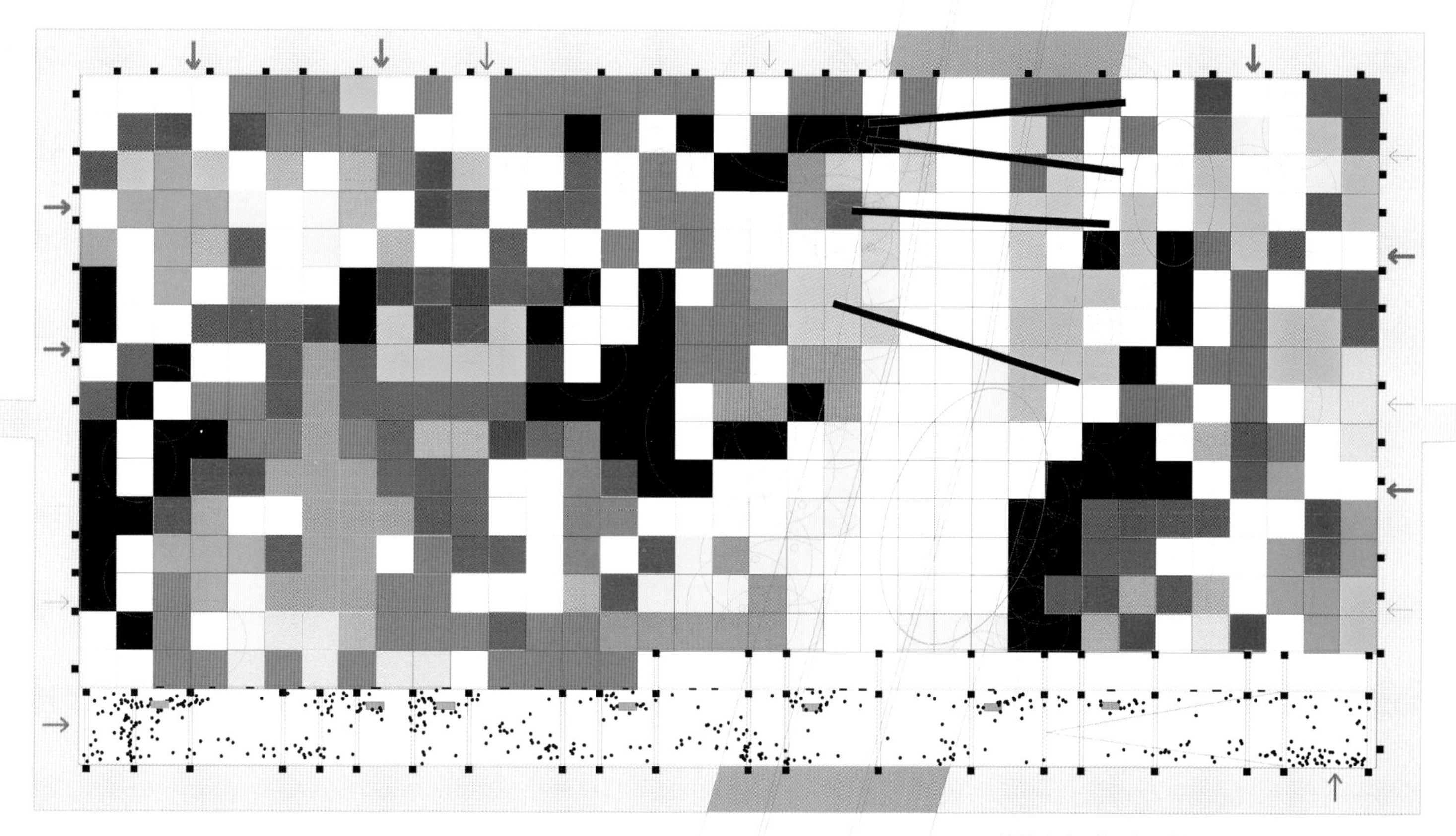

If this is the site plan of the garden, then in what nook or cranny might Jane be hiding?

The answer lies in the very design of the garden, which has been conceived as a pixelated version of Jane's face. The color code shown here corresponds to where certain plant species were placed.

In addition to its function as a physical boundary, the fence also links elements with diverse functions.

Mist rises from the ground and fades into thick bunches of hanging ropes, a forest of vines, in a nearly subterranean environment.

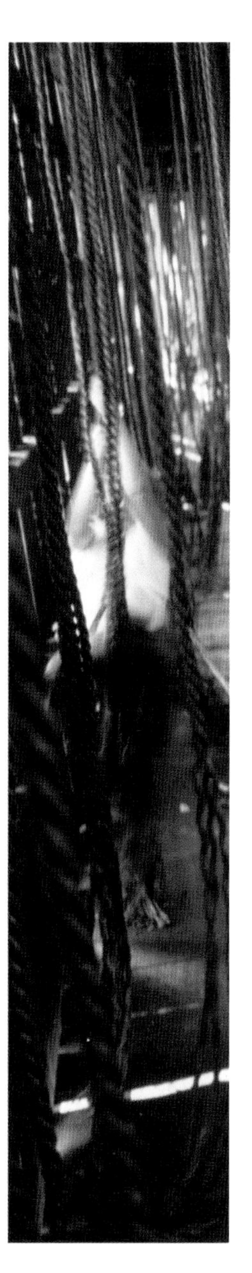

Swings hang from the vines, providing a perfect observation post from which to enjoy the jungle, which disappears into the darkness.

PS 244 Sound Playground

New York City, USA

Bill & Mary
BUCHEN sonicarchitecture

photographs contributed by the designers

Sonic Architecture designed these two playgrounds, which are incorporated into a new wing at PS 244, an elementary school in Brooklyn, to explore music and the physics of acoustic phenomena. Two outdoor sites were selected for the installation: an inner playground (for preschool through second grade) which is enclosed by two and four-story school buildings on all sides, and an outer playground for grades 3-6 bordered on two sides by buildings and on two sides by adjoining streets. The Project met with such success that student enrollment increased from 900 to 1400 when it was completed.

In the playground for older children, groupings of bronze drums engage children in communal music-making and serve a dual function as tables and seats. Five Bata drums of Haitian origin and parabolic dishes in the Drum Circle connect to a large underground chamber. Children hear their voices and playing reverberating through grates in the concrete benches and in the center of the dishes.

In the early childhood play area, children communicate through a network of curvilinear, color-coded "Telephone Tubes" which are interconnected underground.

Flowering vines, bushes and trees surround the fenced peripheries of the playground area to create visual and acoustic isolation from the service area and protect the privacy of the nearby residential zone.

These stainless steel "palm trees" are composed of open-ended tubes that are tuned to a seven note diatonic scale. By listening and speaking into them, children hear the resonant frequency of each pipe.

Conga shaped "talking drums" (Tumba, Conga & Quinto) of Afro-Cuban origin are connected underground by sets of pipes, and are flanked by large parabolic dishes that focus sounds to a central point, where children can hear their own amplified voices.

In the early childhood play area, children communicate through a network of curvilinear, color-coded "telephone tubes" which are interconnected underground. The ends of the tubes, which channel sound from one end to the other, are partially covered by perforated screens.Children can climb all over these painted steel structures which have been built on a safety surface that covers the play area.

Vulkangarten

Ostfildern, Germany

photographs: Andreas Peyker

KNÖLL OKOPLAN

Volcano Park forms part of a complex of installations that are leftover from the gardening tradeshow which took place here in 2002. The motif of this original park is the city's geologic history and volcanic origins.

Contiguous grass-carpeted pyramids delimit the playground, making it a microcosm for children only. Cement cones, water and sand make up an artificial volcanic landscape, with recreated rivers of lava, expanses of ash and solidified lava. Two red, truncated, cement cones of different heights can be used by the children for climbing up and sliding down. The borders of the Volcano Park are covered in dense growth of tamarisks with pink flowers that seem to grow over an extinct lava bed; or at least such is the impression elicited by the basaltic rocks strewn about.

The slope of the volcanoes is gentle enough for kids to be able to climb to the top.

The smallest of the volcanoes is connected to a hydraulic system with a pump that can generate a spout of water of up to five meters in height.

Ground plan of the park. Two "lava rivers" - one sand, the other water - run their separate courses.

The recreation of a volcanic landscape recalls the site's history and enables children to play amongst elements with which they can identify.

HEADS Co., Ltd.

©I. Kanai

©I. Kanai

Akibadai Park

Tama New Town, Tokyo, Japan

Akibadai Park sits on a site where there was once a shrine to honor the god of fire. Thus, the park features certain characteristic elements such as a playground based on the "Bird of Fire" legend. The graceful shape of the bird, laid on gently rolling terrain with a multi-colored recycled stone mosaic pattern, can be best appreciated from the top of the park's pyramid.

The form of a pyramid was chosen as a logical solution in adhering to the natural shape of the hill; it measures 17 meters in height and 70 meters in length at the base. Elegant steps of andesite stone (a material chosen to confer the desired "ancient" look) lead to an observatory, which is lit at night, thereby resembling the glowing eye of a "Rising Dragon". As legend has it, the Rising Dragon was a god of water that roamed the realms of air and water with equal ease. A 17-meter-long "Rising Dragon" slide spills down the front of the pyramid, culminating in a soft sand pit in the very belly of the firebird below.

©I. Kanai

©I. Kanai

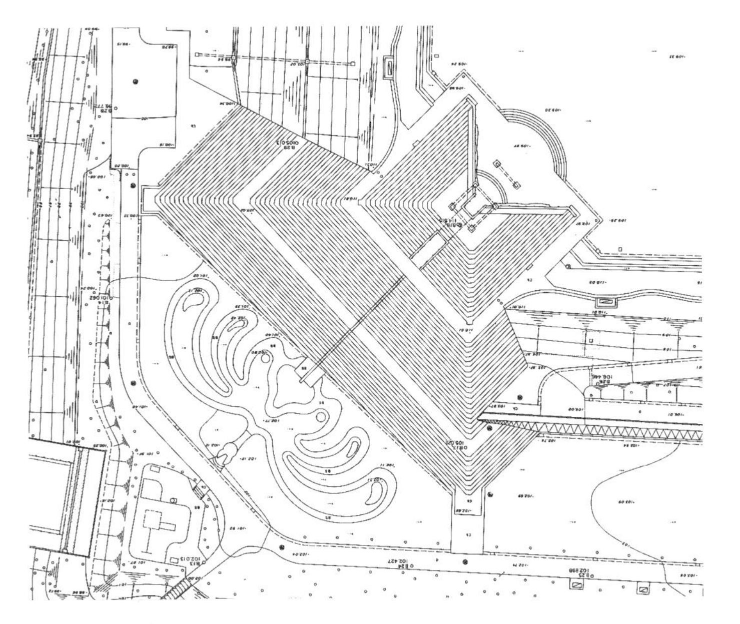

©O. Kato

The graceful shape of a firebird, seen here in the ground plan, is best viewed from the top of the pyramid. Massive steps of andesite stone give the pyramid a stately, aged appearance.

©I. Kanai

©I. Kanai

The "Rising Dragon" slide, measuring 17 meters in length and spanning a difference in level of 8 meters, is a fast, exhilarating ride for the most daring youngsters.

©A. Hirosawa

©I. Kanai

An observatory sits at the top of the pyramid, making this park as popular an attraction at night as by day.

©O. Kato

©I. Kanai

©I. Kanai

The surface of the firebird's wings, which are gently sloped to provide a safe and fun play space for kids, is made up of a mosaic pattern in recycled stone. The Rising Dragon slide empties into a soft sand pit in the belly of the bird.

©I. Kanai

©I. Kanai

©O. Kato

art2architecture

Photographs: Mag.art.Reinhard Bernsteiner

Emslie Horniman Park

London, England

This project involved the total redesign and revitalization of Emslie Horniman Pleasance, a public park located in a particularly deprived neighborhood of North Kensington. The park is now a vital local asset in an area where the ratio of open space to population is by far the lowest in London.

The redesign involved major improvements to the park and its environs along with the restoration of its centerpiece, a listed walled garden by the eminent Arts and Crafts architect, CFA Voysey. Different color-designated areas have been included for organized five-a-side sports, children's activities, a dog run and quiet areas.

The project won the Kensington & Chelsea Environment Award of 1999 and the Britain in Bloom Environmental Improvement Award of 1999.

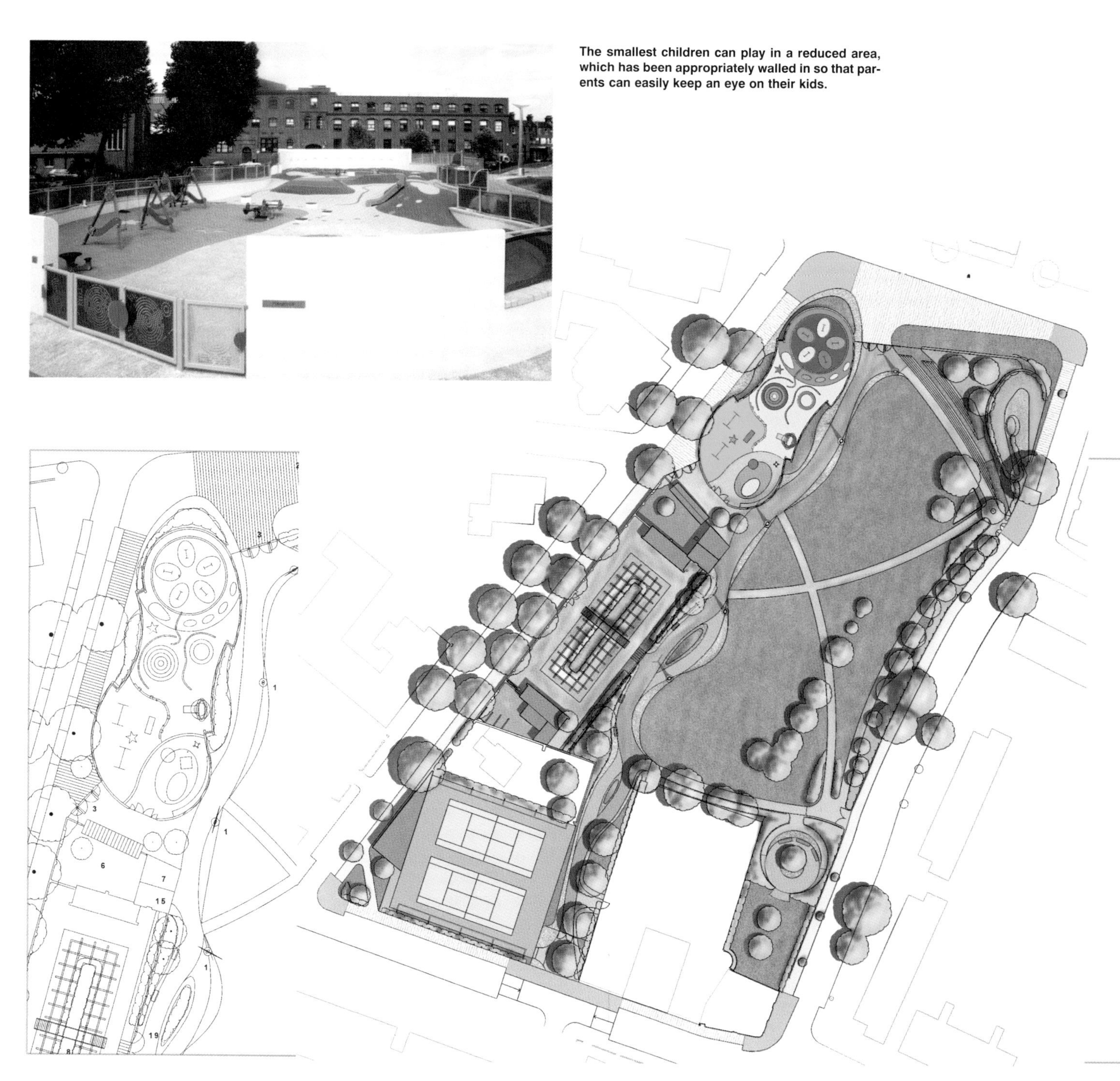

The smallest children can play in a reduced area, which has been appropriately walled in so that parents can easily keep an eye on their kids.

Different areas intended for all age groups have been included in the park, with plenty of space for bicycling and playing ball games.

A thousand different details come together to ensure that every child will find something to suit his or her personality and preferences.

The risk of injury has been reduced to a minimum with these soft rolling hills, which comprise a veritable play paradise for small children.

Westborough Primary School

Westcliff-on-Sea, Essex, England

Cottrell & Vermeulen

photographs contrubuted by the designers

This refurbished playground takes the place of the school's original, inherently problematic one. Prior to this project, the surface was uneven, children were frequently hurt, there were little or no green and planted areas and wheelchair users were unable to negotiate level changes. A scheme was developed with the school to create different environments within the existing space. The bland tarmac desert was changed into a sequence of stimulating spaces designed to accommodate different activities. Within a tight budget sport and play areas were introduced, covered dining and play areas were built on log columns, walls and playground areas were painted and different surface textures, such as rubberized and woven surfaces, were incorporated. A new planting scheme also introduced color and a sense of change to the environment. Although the available space is limited, the planting has been incorporated into the new structures and on vertical surfaces. A project is currently underway for a play structure that will be enveloped in a 'forest canopy' and that will be fully accessible to wheelchairs.

All tarmac surfaces bear painted markings, which serve to visually break up the space into smaller zones as well as to demarcate the boundaries of a game, for example, or to indicate directions.

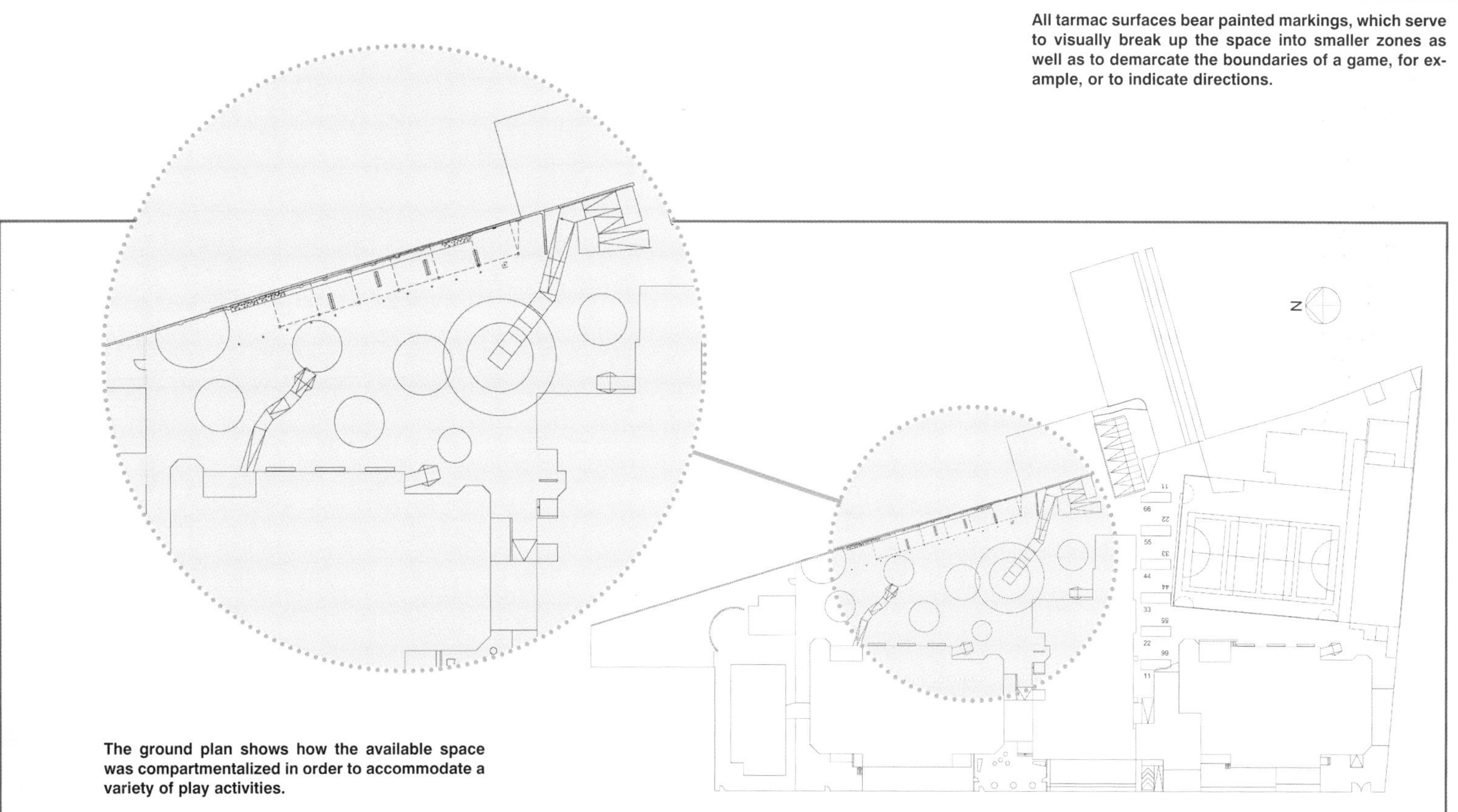

The ground plan shows how the available space was compartmentalized in order to accommodate a variety of play activities.

The ball play area is bounded by colorful walls and, on one side, a chain link separation to keep stray balls from bouncing into the covered walkway. (The photograph above was taken before the ground markings indicating different games and areas were painted.)

55
44

A wide variety of activities has been included to suit all preferences: a "musical screen" made from polyethylene gas pipes has been included in the ball play area.

A crosswalk becomes an educational game and a whimsical play spot made from recycled rubber provides a padded surface for whatever game the imagination can conjure.

A vertical planting wall (which the children actively help to maintain) and an awning for shade provide the perfect place for the kids to have their lunch break.

An external deck provides access to the classrooms. Here, a lunchbox storage wall becomes a colorful installation in itself.

Parc de l'Espanya Industrial

Barcelona, Spain

Andrés Nagel photographs: Joan Argelés

Inspired by the legend of Saint George, this imposing dragon sits at the north entrance to the Parc de l'Espanya Industrial, a recreation area occupying the site of a defunct 19th century textile factory (which also lent its name to the current park). The design was conceived by the Basque artist Andrés Nagel and was installed shortly after the park was inaugurated.
Kids can enter this cast iron dragon and climb to the highest point, where they find the openings to three enormous slides that shoot down the wings and head, ending up at its giant open mouth. This sculpture is an endless source of fun for children and also serves as a lookout point with unobstructed views of the park lying at its feet.
A recent renovation has brought safety regulations up to date and has returned this iron dragon to the splendor it enjoyed before vandalism once tarnished its appearance.

These ramp-like slides not only captivate small children, but also lure the most daring skaters.

The dragon's imposing tail arches dramatically before dipping toward its resting place in the artificial lake that cools the park.

The dragon's enormous silhouette is that much more imposing when viewed up close, when each of the iron pieces is starkly outlined against the backdrop of the city and the vaulted sky.

Urban Treehouse

New York City, USA

photographs contributed by the designers

Chermayeff & Geismar

The Urban Tree House, which opened on Earth Day 1992, is constructed from pieces of the city - traffic cones, a water tower and steel girders. This unique 20,000-square-foot exhibit was conceived to enliven the museum's courtyard and provide kids with a new perspective of natural and urban cycles. Children are encouraged to participate. By being able to lift a week's worth of garbage, for example, a comparison between NYC daily trash (45 lbs due to high consumption and limited recycling) and Tokyo (6.5 lbs due to reduced packaging and intensive recycling) are dramatized. Children can also learn about wild animals or poke through a cross-section of cables and sewer pipes.
The New York Times noted in its extensive review that "the structure involves children with hands-on, entertaining experience where they can really learn the lessons of reduce, recycle, re-use and re-think."

Children feel, by lifting it, how much garbage is generated by the average family in a day or a week.

Children and adults alike participate in workshops where they create something new from recycled materials or learn about water and soil cycles.

Mi-fog, acting as air conditioning during the summer, gives out a fine mist to the delight of children playing at a stream table below it.

Hormigas

Platja d'Aro, Spain

Martirià Figueras

Photographs contributed by Martirià Figueras

This project came about with the proposal to landscape the exterior of the local sanitation company's pump station in Abat Escarrer Plaza. The scheme combined the desire to create a common, yet symbolic, space with that of winning the acceptance of the townspeople. It also had to be successfully integrated into the surrounding area, unifying the diverse existing spaces while also creating something new and distinct.

Figueras struck upon the idea of the ant to fulfill these criteria and then set about giving it form with the suitable material. Since then, eight giant polyester ants have taken over the plaza, walkway chimney stacks and parking lot. These whimsical sculptures are fun for children and represent something unique in a space which previously provided very little food for the imagination.

Measuring 1.8 meters in length, the ants are built from colored polyester covered in transparent resin.

The design generates mobility in order to spatially conquer the site: the play equipment visually interacts with the plaza and with the people strolling by on the abutting avenue.

The dual interactive capacity of these fantastic insects is based on their being play equipment for children by day and lamps by night.

Taylor Cullity Lethlean

Photographs contributed by the designers

Hemmings Park

Dandenong, Australia

Hemmings Park is a large, custom-built regional adventure playground with a variety of activities which were based on Dandenong's history in the timber industry and on images of local migrant children from non-English speaking cultures. The project involved extensive community consultation, especially with local children. This consultation was designed to tap into the experiences and imagination of Dandenong's rich array of ethnic cultures.

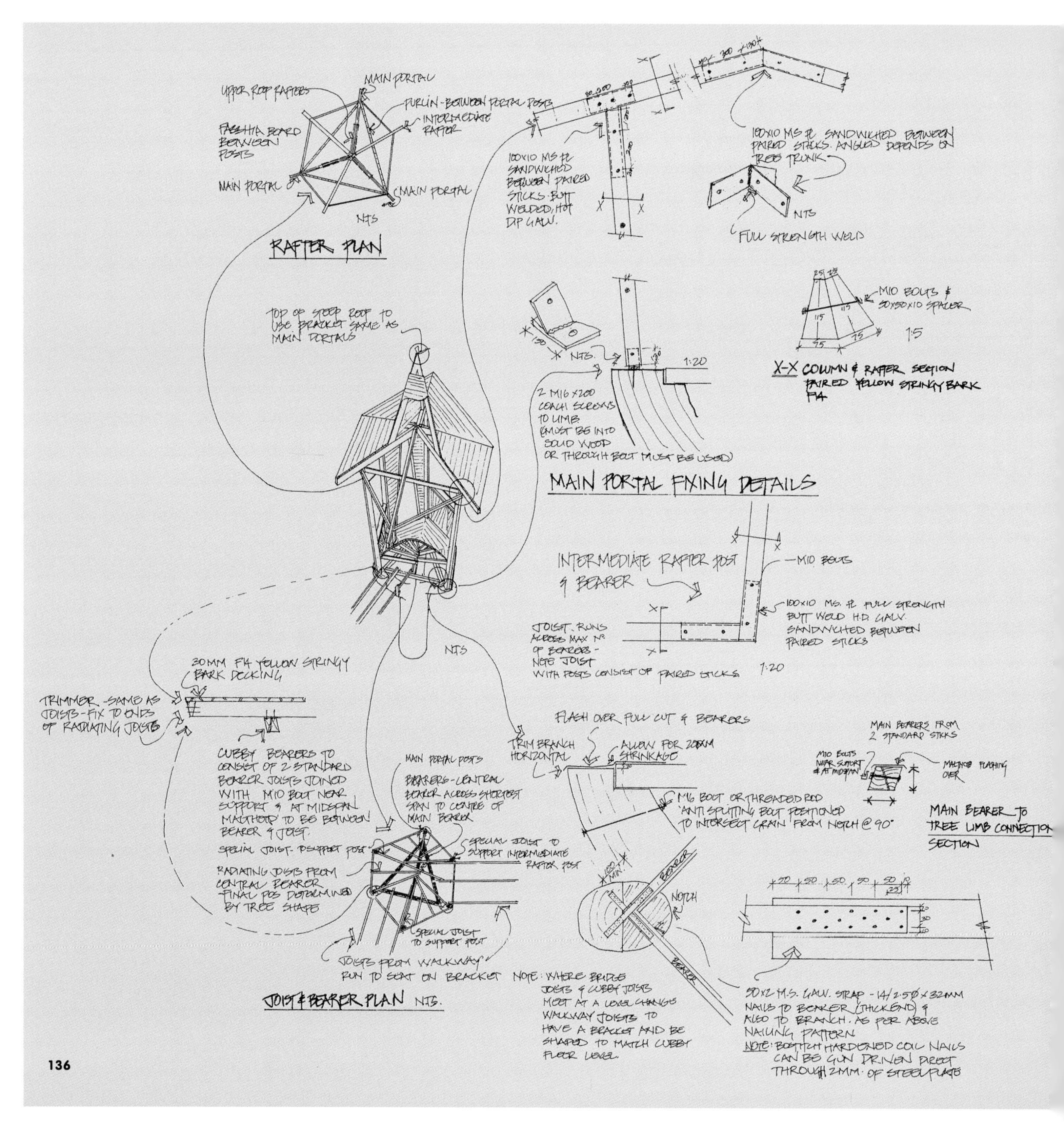

UPPER ROOF RAFTERS
MAIN PORTAL
PURLIN-BETWEEN PORTAL POSTS
INTERMEDIATE RAFTER
FASCIA BOARD BETWEEN POSTS
MAIN PORTAL
MAIN PORTAL
NTS
RAFTER PLAN
100x10 MS PL SANDWICHED BETWEEN PAIRED STICKS-BUTT WELDED, HOT DIP GALV.
100x10 MS PL SANDWICHED BETWEEN PAIRED STICKS. ANGLED DEPENDS ON TREE TRUNK
NTS
FULL STRENGTH WELD
TOP OF STEEP ROOF TO USE BRACKET SAME AS MAIN PORTALS
NTS
1:20
2 M16 x200 COACH SCREWS TO LIMB (MUST BE INTO SOLID WOOD OR THROUGH BOLT MUST BE USED)
M10 BOLTS & 50x50x10 SPACER
1:5
X-X COLUMN & RAFTER SECTION PAIRED YELLOW STRINGYBARK F14
MAIN PORTAL FIXING DETAILS
INTERMEDIATE RAFTER POST & BEARER
M10 BOLTS
100x10 MS PL FULL STRENGTH BUTT WELD H.D. GALV. SANDWICHED BETWEEN PAIRED STICKS
JOIST RUNS ACROSS MAX No OF BEARERS - NOTE JOIST WITH POSTS CONSIST OF PAIRED STICKS
1:20
NTS
30MM F14 YELLOW STRINGY BARK DECKING
TRIMMER -SAME AS JOISTS-FIX TO ENDS OF RADIATING JOISTS
CUBBY BEARERS TO CONSIST OF 2 STANDARD BEARER JOISTS JOINED WITH M10 BOLT NEAR SUPPORT & AT MIDSPAN. MALTHOID TO BE BETWEEN BEARER & JOIST.
MAIN PORTAL POSTS
BEARERS-CENTRAL BEARER ACROSS SHORTEST SPAN TO CENTRE OF MAIN BEARER
SPECIAL JOIST- TO SUPPORT POST
SPECIAL JOIST TO SUPPORT INTERMEDIATE RAFTER POST
RADIATING JOISTS FROM CENTRAL BEARER FINAL POS DETERMINED BY TREE SHAPE
SPECIAL JOIST TO SUPPORT POST
JOISTS FROM WALKWAY RUN TO SEAT ON BRACKET
JOIST & BEARER PLAN NTS.
NOTE: WHERE BRIDGE JOISTS & CUBBY JOISTS MEET AT A LEVEL CHANGE WALKWAY JOISTS TO HAVE A BRACKET AND BE SHAPED TO MATCH CUBBY FLOOR LEVEL.
FLASH OVER FULL CUT & BEARERS
TRIM BRANCH HORIZONTAL
ALLOW FOR 20MM SHRINKAGE
M16 BOLT OR THREADED ROD ANTI SPLITTING BOLT POSITIONED TO INTERSECT GRAIN FROM NOTCH @ 90°
MAIN BEARERS FROM 2 STANDARD STICKS
M10 BOLTS NEAR SUPPORT & AT MIDSPAN
MALTHOID FLASHING OVER
MAIN BEARER TO TREE LIMB CONNECTION SECTION
BEARER
NOTCH
BEARER
50x2 M.S. GALV. STRAP - 14/2.5Ø x 32MM NAILS TO BEARER (THICK END) & ALSO TO BRANCH. AS PER ABOVE NAILING PATTERN
NOTE: BOSTITCH HARDENED COIL NAILS CAN BE GUN DRIVEN DIRECT THROUGH 2MM. OF STEEL PLATE

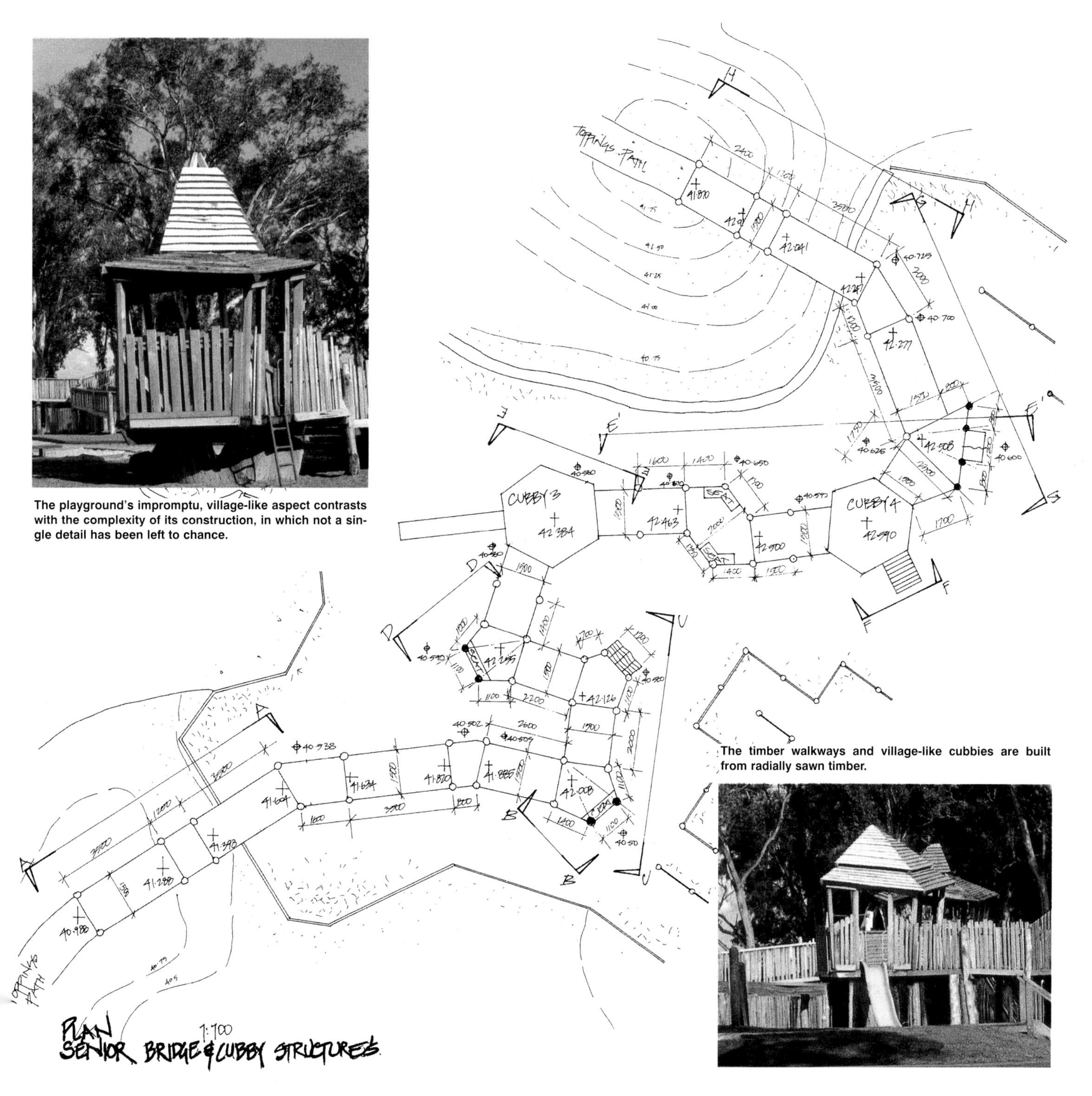

The playground's impromptu, village-like aspect contrasts with the complexity of its construction, in which not a single detail has been left to chance.

The timber walkways and village-like cubbies are built from radially sawn timber.

Slides and ladders have been added to the cubbies, which are in and of themselves highly attractive and stimulating structures for children.

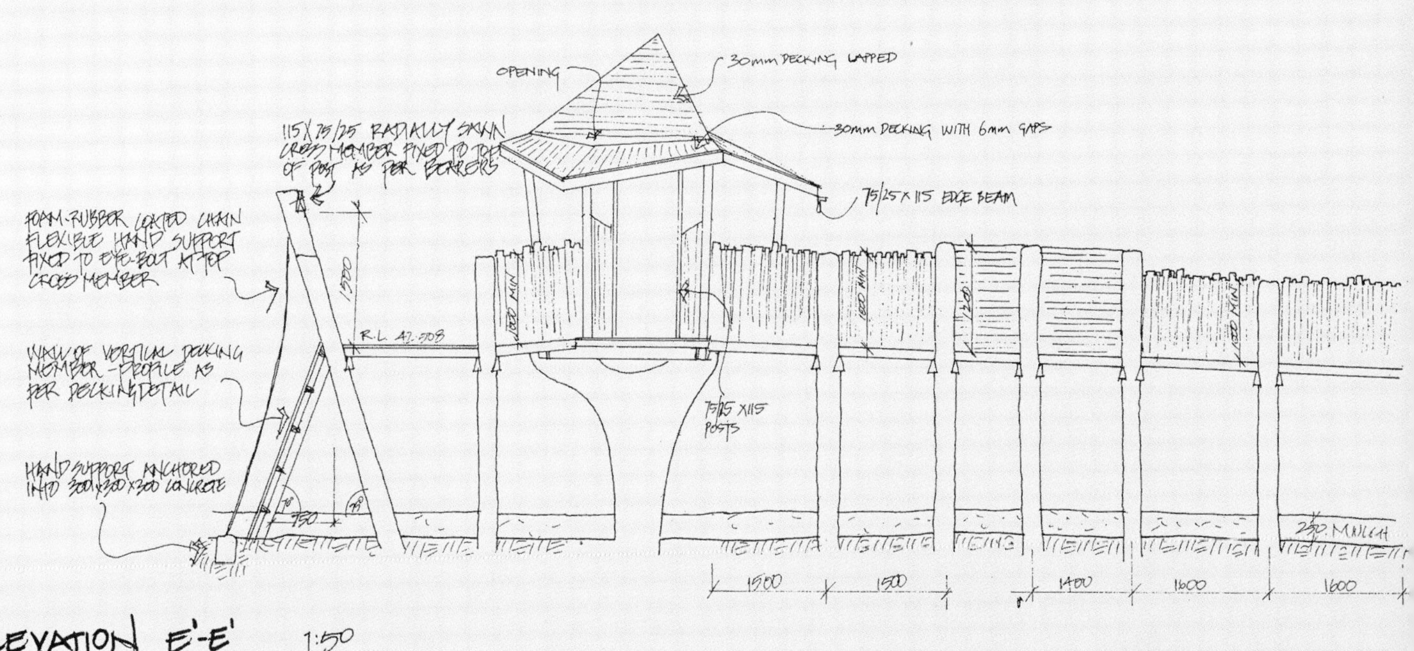

The playground of elevated timber decks and village like cubbies is set among mature gum trees. It has been designed to be fully accessible to the disabled.

PS23 Sound Playground

New York City, USA

Bill & Mary BUCHEN
sonicarchitecture

photographs contributed by the designers

This permanent sound installation at P.S. 23, a Bronx elementary school, was commissioned by the NYC Percent for Art Program. Sonic Architecture designed the entire playground, including sound sculptures, paving, seating and landscaping.
Everything revolves around sound and rhythm in this playground, where we find drum seats, parabolic elements for amplifying sound and tables for experimenting with rhythm and creating music. Even the fence surrounding the school is mounted with bells that chime in the wind.

The Big Eyes-Big Ears rotating tower, which extends the user's listening and viewing capabilities via parabolic dishes and a periscope.

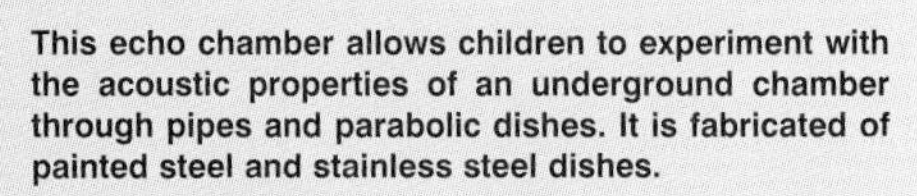

This echo chamber allows children to experiment with the acoustic properties of an underground chamber through pipes and parabolic dishes. It is fabricated of painted steel and stainless steel dishes.

Not only are these nine stools perfect for creating rhythm with percussion, they also from a sculptural grouping of great plastic beauty.

Playing at making music is more fun when done with a group of friends. This table and chair set for experimenting with percussion and rhythm was designed for just such a collective experience.

This pair of benches with stainless steel parabolic dishes measuring nearly two and a half meters in diameter creates an acoustic space for reflecting and focusing sound. Children discover they can generate sound waves and then stop them with a wave of the hand.

Fliegergarten

Ostfildern, Germany

KNÖLL OKOPLAN photographs: Andreas Peyker

This "aviation" park recalls the site's past: it was used for several decades by the Nazis as a military flight camp and, later, by the American army until well into the 1990s. Here visitors find the evocation of an airport, with abstractions of a landing strip, control tower and heliport.
The installation emits a somewhat hardened, industrial air, as the design has left out any elements that might soften it or make it explicitly "for children". In fact, this recreation area has been specifically designed for the bigger kids and adolescents, who do not often find spaces or equipment that match their level of ability or that offer a challenge.

The control tower reaches a height of eight meters and can be scaled using the climbing nets. The tallest slide is six meters high.

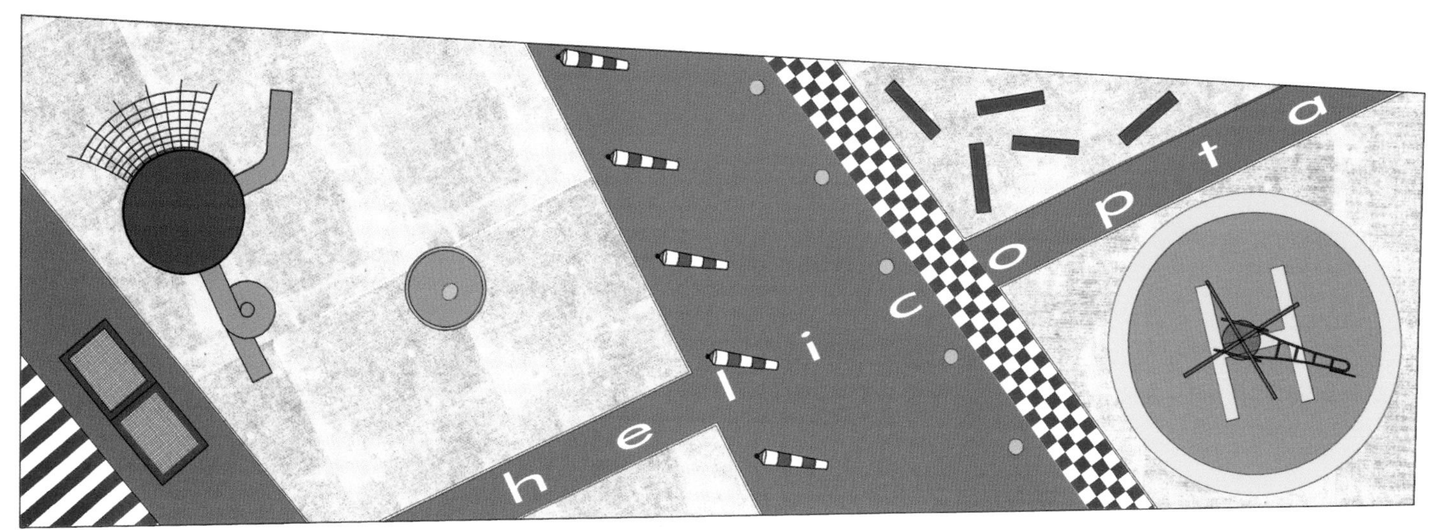

Ground plan of the park. The paving consists primarily of sand and gravel; the runways are paved in concrete.

The structure of this helicopter made from circular tubes is sturdy enough to be climbed all over. Inside the pilot's cabin, there are two seats and control levers so kids can play at "make believe".

Fog Forest

Tachikawa City, Tokyo, Japan

Atsugi Kitawagara Architects Inc.

photographs: Sigeo Ogawa

©Shigeo Ogawa

The Atsushi Kitagawara team and the artist Fujiko Nakaya, known for her fog sculptures, worked together to bring about this exceptional "Fog Forest", which evokes the image of a mythical landscape ensconced in an aura of magic and mystery.
A large perforated steel tube pours a variable flow of artificial fog across an unusual landscape of truncated pyramids. The dense barrier of trees and bushes that defines the perimeter of the park is a contrast to the regularly placed pyramids, which take on the appearance of a large-scale texture stamped onto the natural setting.
The wind gently filtered through the forest canopy disperses the fog across the landscape so that the overall look of the place changes with each passing moment. When the breeze is calm, the place is covered in a blanket of clouds. The atmosphere created by the shapeless mass of fog over the contours of the terrain, which pacifies the wind and traps the fog, shows visitors an image of extraordinary, almost dreamlike, beauty.

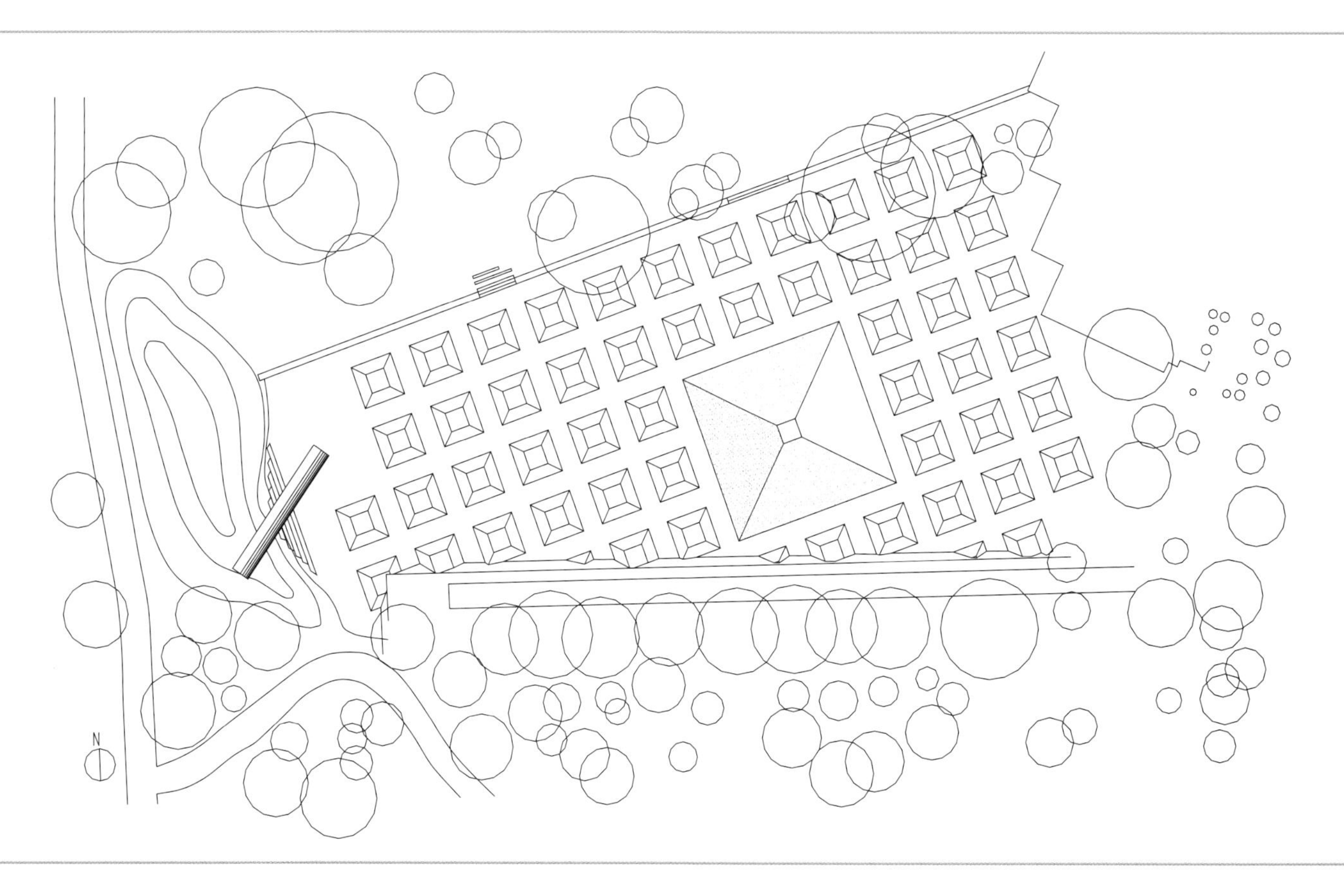

The ground plan shows the outline of truncated pyramids amidst the vegetation, with the fog-generating tube to the left and the fog "lake" in the center.

A ten-meter-long tube sits at one end of the site and encases a high-tech fog-generating mechanism, which was designed by Fujiko Nakaya herself. The pumps kick in every 15 minutes and generate a stream of fog with a varying rate of flow and volume.

For this project, the artist conducted a series of experiments with fog in a wind tunnel in order to determine the characteristics of the perforations along the tube for producing air movement.

Children "plunge into" the "lake", play hide-and-seek, appear, disappear, imagine shapes. This element does not respond to touch, it emerges, flows, rises, floats at ground level or evaporates into thin air, creating the impression of a fantastical, unreal atmosphere that fascinates children and suggests an endless variety of games.

Below, one of the project's initial models took on this suggestive aspect.

©Shigeo Ogawa

Kinnear Landscape Architects

photographs contributed by the architects

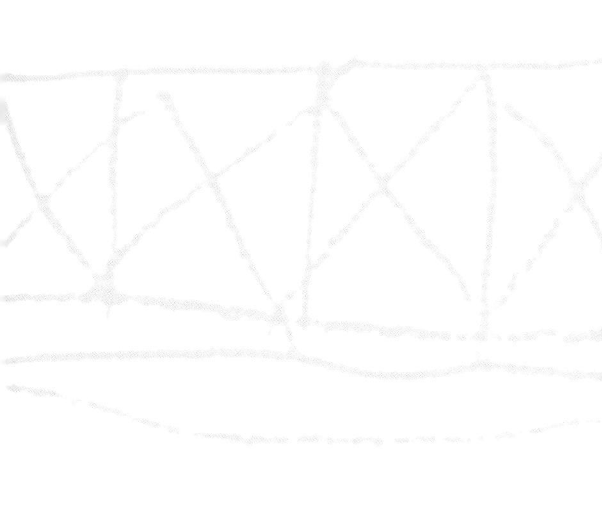

Helling Street Park

London, UK

This small urban park designed to accommodate recreational sports and activities was developed after evaluating input from the local community and the adjacent school. The design is defined by the layout of a colorful artificial landscape and by the clear compartmentalization of the play areas, which include swings and a rope structure for climbing, artificial fiber glass rocks and a wooden fort. A thick, bright blue wall divides the playground from the more peaceful area where adults can relax under a canopy of pine trees.
The park as a whole is separated from the urban surroundings by shrubs cut to varying heights and walls that conform to even the steepest slopes. This is just one more special detail in the midst of a true urban oasis made up of simple components and a liberal dose of the imagination.

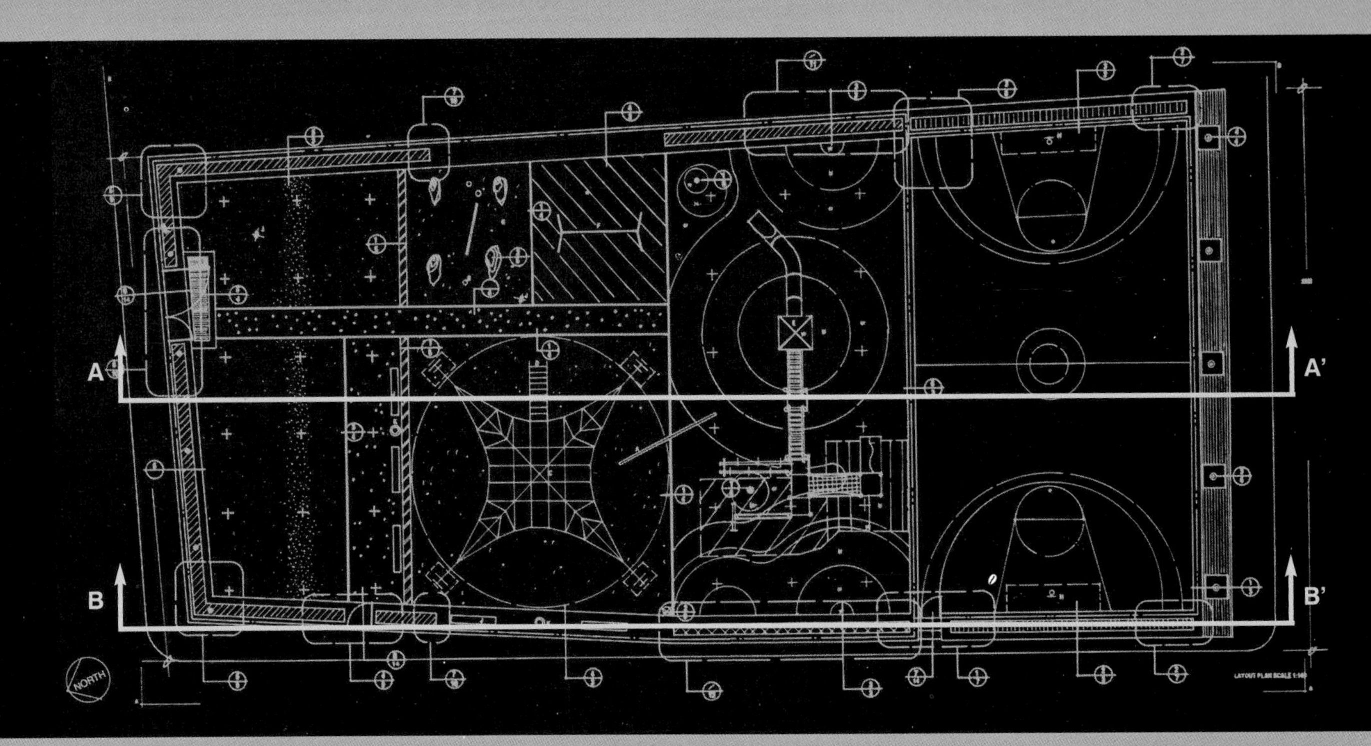

The ground plan shows a clear compartmentalization of the play areas.

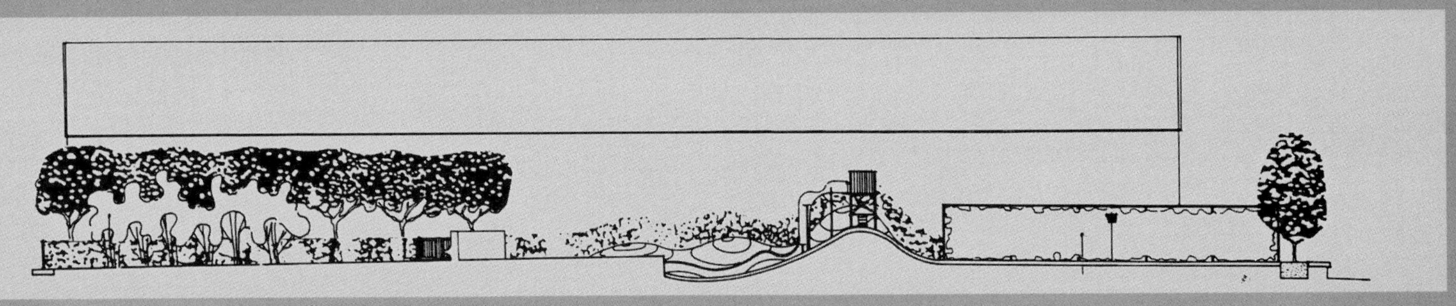

Longitudinal section A-A'.

Longitudinal section B-B'.

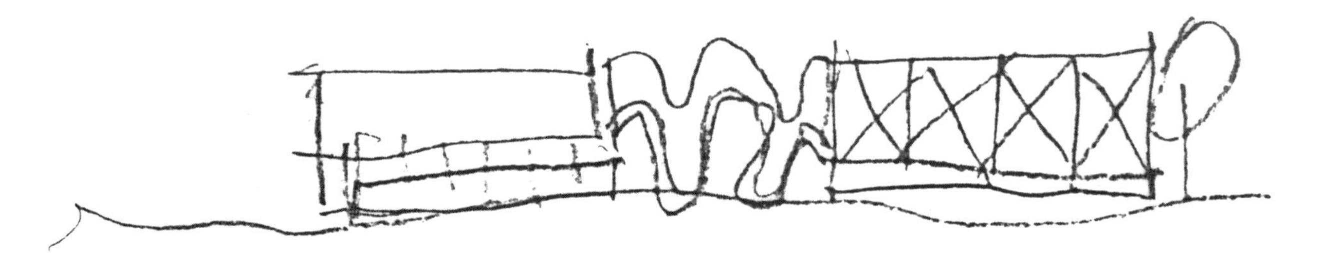

The park's unusual surface was conceived as a plane pushed to its limits.

This undulating landscape is an excellent resource for optimizing the possibilities where ground space is limited.

Color, which enriches the contours of the landscape, is a central, defining element in this project.

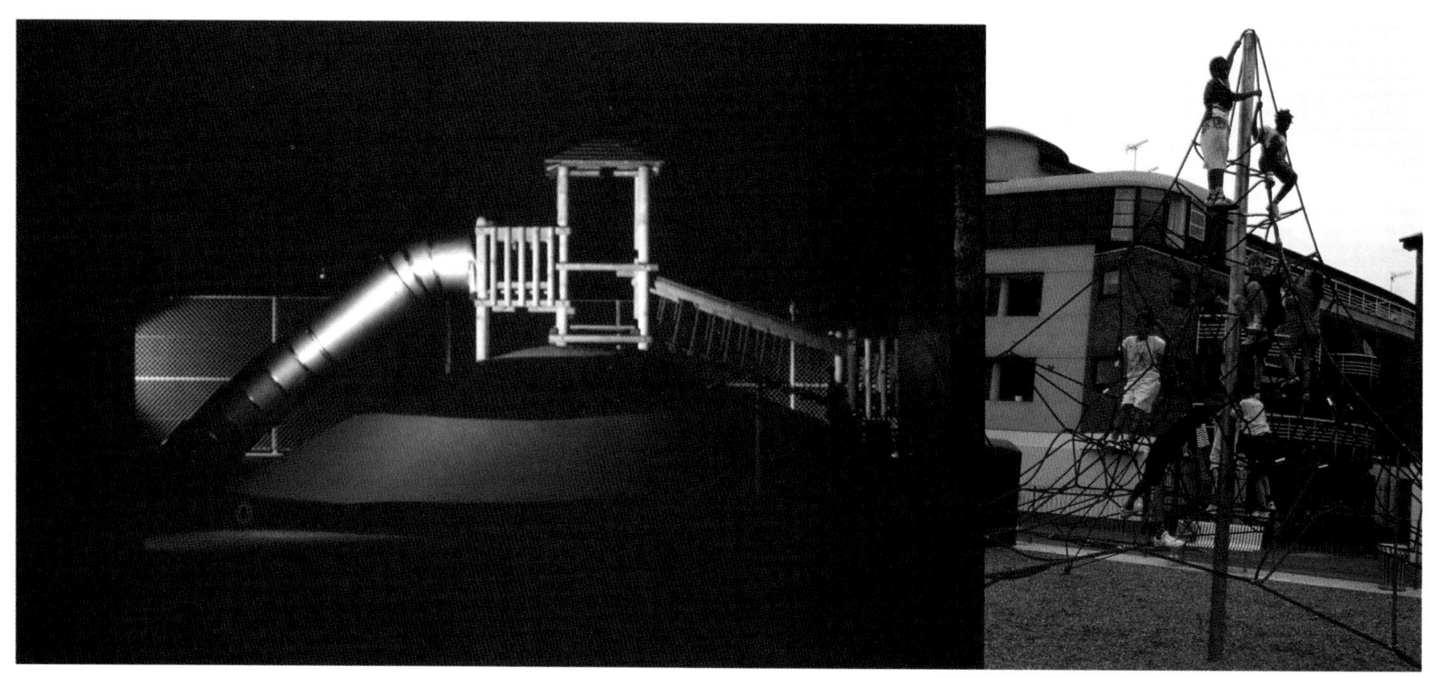

The spaces change from night to day, with the galvanized finishes reflecting the light cast by the lampposts.

In the photo to the right, notice the ground tree bark spread beneath the climbing net in order to pad possible falls.

Greg Healey

Jimmy Melrose Park

Adelaide, Australia

©Don Brice

The Jimmy Melrose Park project was a major upgrade of a strip of coastal park at Glenelg, a premier tourist coastal precinct in Adelaide, South Australia. The upgrade included these cheerful play bollards, which are a symbolic reference to the "real" bollards that serve to moor vessels in the nearby harbor. The intention of the play bollards was to mark the entrance to the park and to engage the creative imagination of children and adults alike as they walk by. Made from mild steel, they have been painted in bright colors to create a joyful, exuberant and fun appearance. They range in height from one meter to one and half meters.

Helle Nebelong

Photographs: **Helle Nebelong**

Valbyparken
Copenhagen, Denmark

It is surprising to learn that Valbyparken, now Denmark's largest park, occupies the site of a former garbage dump. The land has been thoroughly cleaned up and renovated, while the earth from the dump was put to use in forming a row of hills separating the playground from the rest of the park.

Nebelong believes that children, being constantly surrounded by color and movement, should be given the opportunity to rest their eyes and minds when playing outside; therefore, natural colors are the most appropriate. Indeed, the simple and natural components of this park have a calming effect and are particularly suited to awakening a sense of curiosity and fantasy, suggesting a variety of adventures and challenges. Thus, this fully natural playground provides an excellent alternative to the many synthetic parks that have sprung up on the urban landscape.

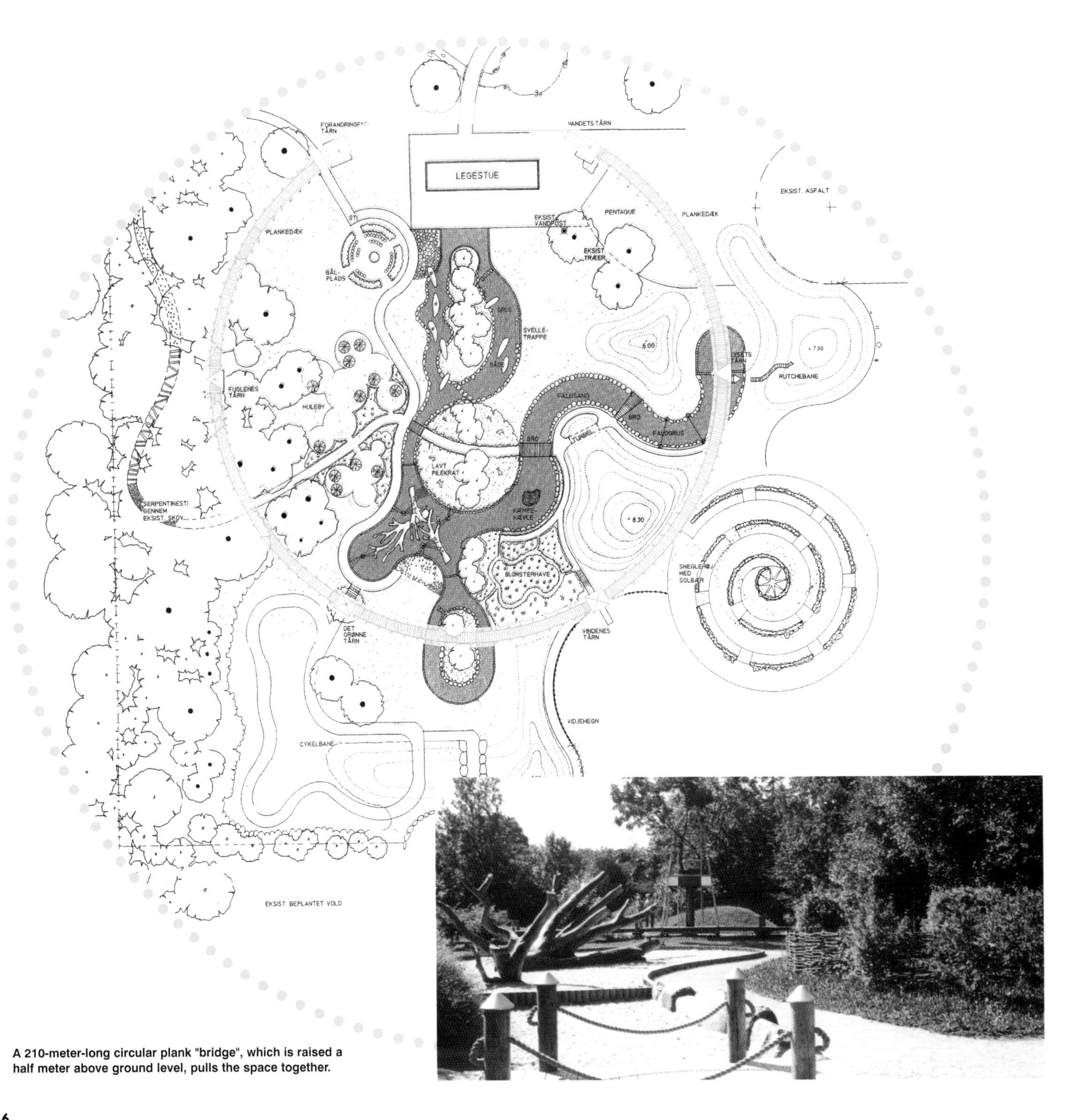

A 210-meter-long circular plank "bridge", which is raised a half meter above ground level, pulls the space together.

The playground is made up solely of organic elements, such as this village of woven willow huts and plaited fences.

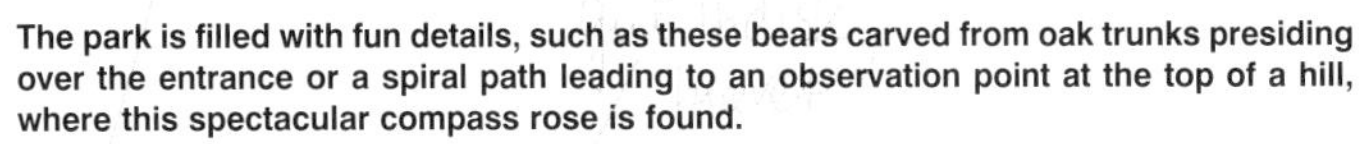

The park is filled with fun details, such as these bears carved from oak trunks presiding over the entrance or a spiral path leading to an observation point at the top of a hill, where this spectacular compass rose is found.

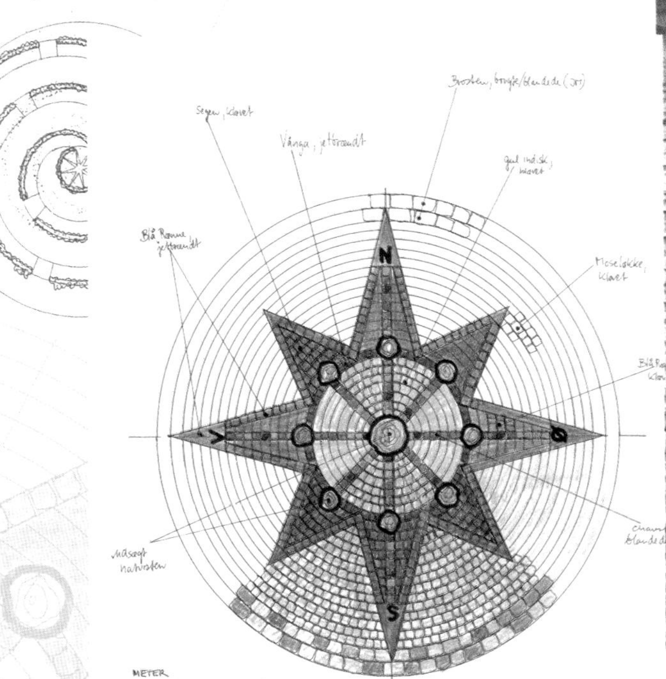

"The Tower of Light"

"The Tower of Change"

Hidden amidst thick foliage, "The Tower of the Birds".

Towers representing diverse motifs designed by students from the School of Design of Denmark are set at six precise points along the bridge. Here we see "The Green Tower".

"The Water Tower", with its undulating, organic shape, rises from the natural terrain like something straight out of a fairy tale.

"The Light Tower" incorporates splashes of color, which are nonetheless only visible from the inside, thereby not affecting the predominant natural tones of the rest of the park.

The cycle of changing seasons has become another aspect of the park itself. The park's trees and plants undergo a series of cyclical changes from spring to autumn.

A large patch of sand and gravel, little green islands, winding paths and a river of sand all compose a suggestive scene where an infinity of adventures might take place. Where to start?

Trunks which had to be felled because of a plague of Dutch elm disease have here been recycled and put to good use as climbing elements, seats, bridges, boats and fences.

Shonadai Cultural Center Fujisawa, Japan

Itsuko Hasegawa photographs Shuji Yamada, Itsuko Hasegawa Atelier

The Shonadai Cultural Center occupies a large, open-air site which the local community has for many years used for various activities, from summer festivals to picnics and sporting events. The architect Itsuko Hasegawa wanted to create the appropriate setting for preserving and enhancing these activities. Thus, in the course of the design competition, the architect referred to concepts such as "architecture as topography", a new kind of environmental design concerned with regionalism, Mother Earth, ancestral rural landscapes and cosmic relations. Hasegawa held various meetings with the local community during the design process in to order to ensure an architecture based on community participation in the project, rather than leaving it to be dealt with in some bureaucratic realm.
Another of Hasegawa's concepts that arose in the design of the center is that of "architecture as latent nature". Like architecture and society, nature and humankind are not mutually exclusive; rather, they come together to create a better environment. This inclusive approximation to architecture is also expressed in the open character of this project's infrastructure and the free flow of paths and roads around the site.

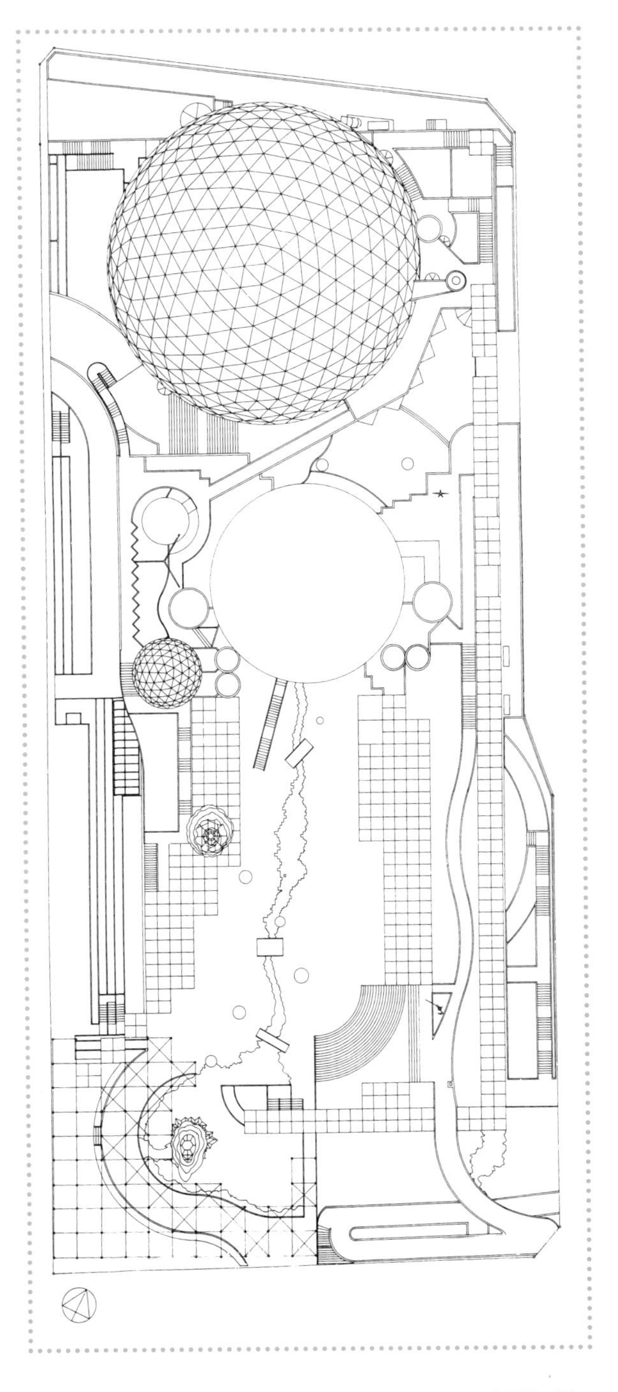

In keeping with the concept of "architecture as latent nature", 70% of the built surface is at below ground level in order to save the greatest amount of space possible for the exterior gardens.

"Architecture as topography" is reflected in the wish to draw tradition and the natural setting into the design scheme.

Children can play with the water in this artificial brook, which is spanned at various points by a series of bridges.

Parc de Sceaux

Paris, France

atelier de launay

photographs contributed by the designers

Because of the strong historical identity of the area surrounding the Parque de Sceaux, the Atelier de Launay team has come up with a design that narrates the town's history. Notions of art, history and landscape are easily perceived and integrated into play activities via five spaces especially adapted to the children's different age groups. Thus, on either side of the main path, visitors come upon spaces with such names as "Edification", which evokes the park in Colbert's time, "Culture", inspired by the era of Voltaire and Lully, "War and Peace", recalling the period between the French Revolution and the First World War, "Reconstruction" and "Present and Future".
Each stopping point on the route therefore represents a specific activity and also enables visitors to gradually learn about the site's history.

Large sculpted pieces of solid wood comprise the play equipment, which may take on the form of books and shelves or animals and diverse figures scattered throughout the various themed areas.

The entrance "unfolds" like the pages of the book that will tell the story of this place.

"Culture" is a play area designed for kids from between 6 and 8 years of age. Letters and musical notes form climbing supports for hands and feet. Kids can also climb around on the shelves of Voltaire's library in this area.

The solid sequoia, cedar, iroko and oak wood comprising the play equipment has been polished and varnished, conferring a noble aspect that highlights its sculptural qualities.

This space is intended for children between 3 and 5 years of age; they can test their balance, climb, jump and slide off of each unique piece.

Five armchairs in solid wood represent five furniture styles from 1700 to 1950.

This large structure rises from the surrounding vegetation in the "Reconstruction" area, which is intended for kids from 9 to 12 years of age.

"Reconstruction" is a space designed to encourage movement and improve balance and strength. The play equipment itself symbolizes scaffolding in large-scale construction work.

Takano Landscape Planning Co., Ltd.

photographs: Takano Landscape Planning

Takino Suzuran Hills Park

Hokkaido, Japan

Takano Landscape's primary concern when designing this park was that children nowadays are increasingly distanced from the natural world and their knowledge of nature, being acquired in school, cannot be transmitted into real life experience. Thus, the design team of this unique park took as inspiration a multitude of natural phenomena, from anthills, beehives and termite nests to hanging nests, underground burrows, spider webs and natural sculptural forms found in caves. Ideas such as "earth", giver of life, or "nest", as home and refuge, have been incorporated into the park as design elements that are open to exploration.

The park is a landscaped area made up of a series of spaces connected by footpaths which are meant to encourage playing in a natural setting in a way that is fun as well as didactic. All of this takes place in the choice setting of Hokkaido, an area of Japan that still enjoys large tracts of natural terrain.

Nijinosu dome&net

Arizuka tower

Arinosu tunnel

Torinosu deck

Forest corridor

Interconnected tunnels and galleries perforate the park throughout its entire area. In the "Arinosu Tunnel" (ant colony), children can roam through the interior and imagine the underground lives of ants or prairie dogs in their dens.

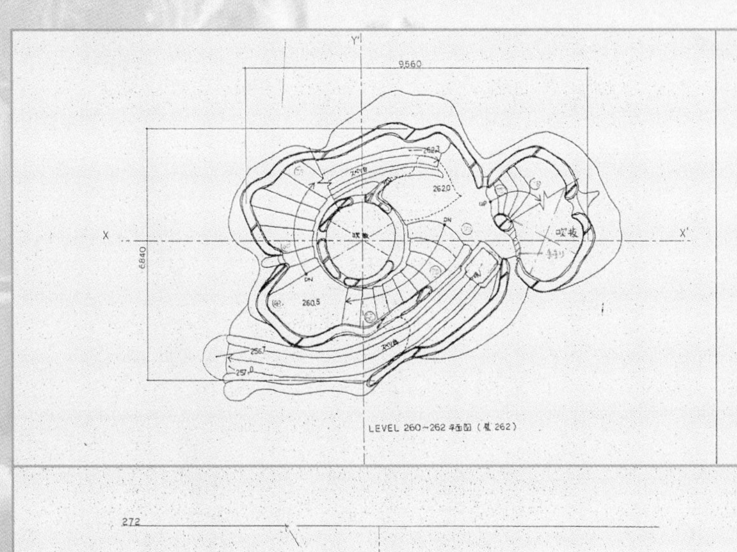

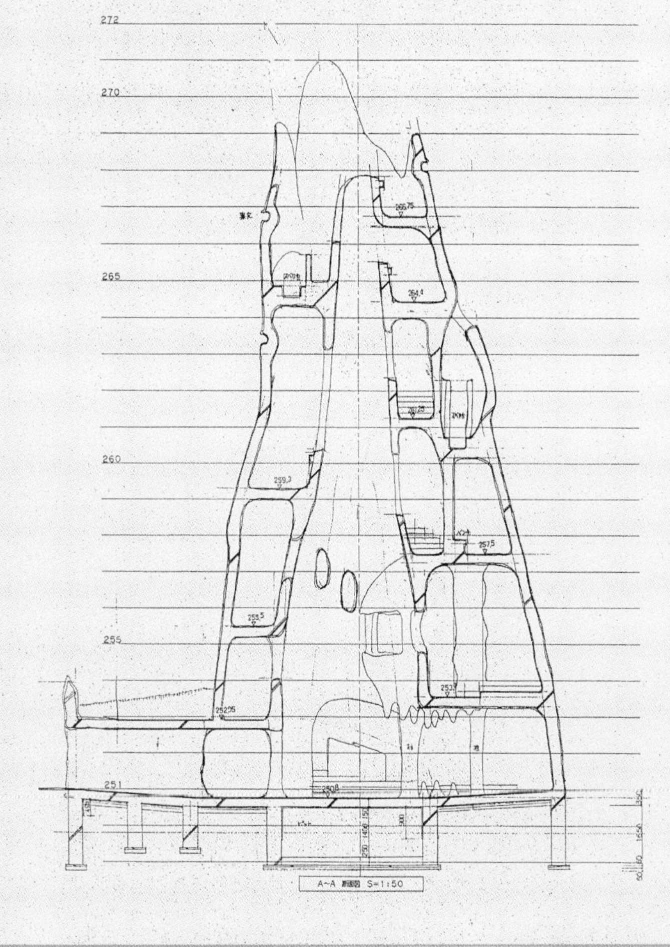

The "Arizuka Tower" (ant hill) is erected over a mound in the manner of a large natural structure; inside, children can feel like small insects. This structure also emulates the air circulation system seen in real ant hills.

The light inside the ant hill has been carefully studied. Just enough is filtered through strategic openings to allow children to find their way comfortably, while an air of mystery still prevails.

Nijinosu, a large egg-shaped cave, is another one of the exceptional points in this park.

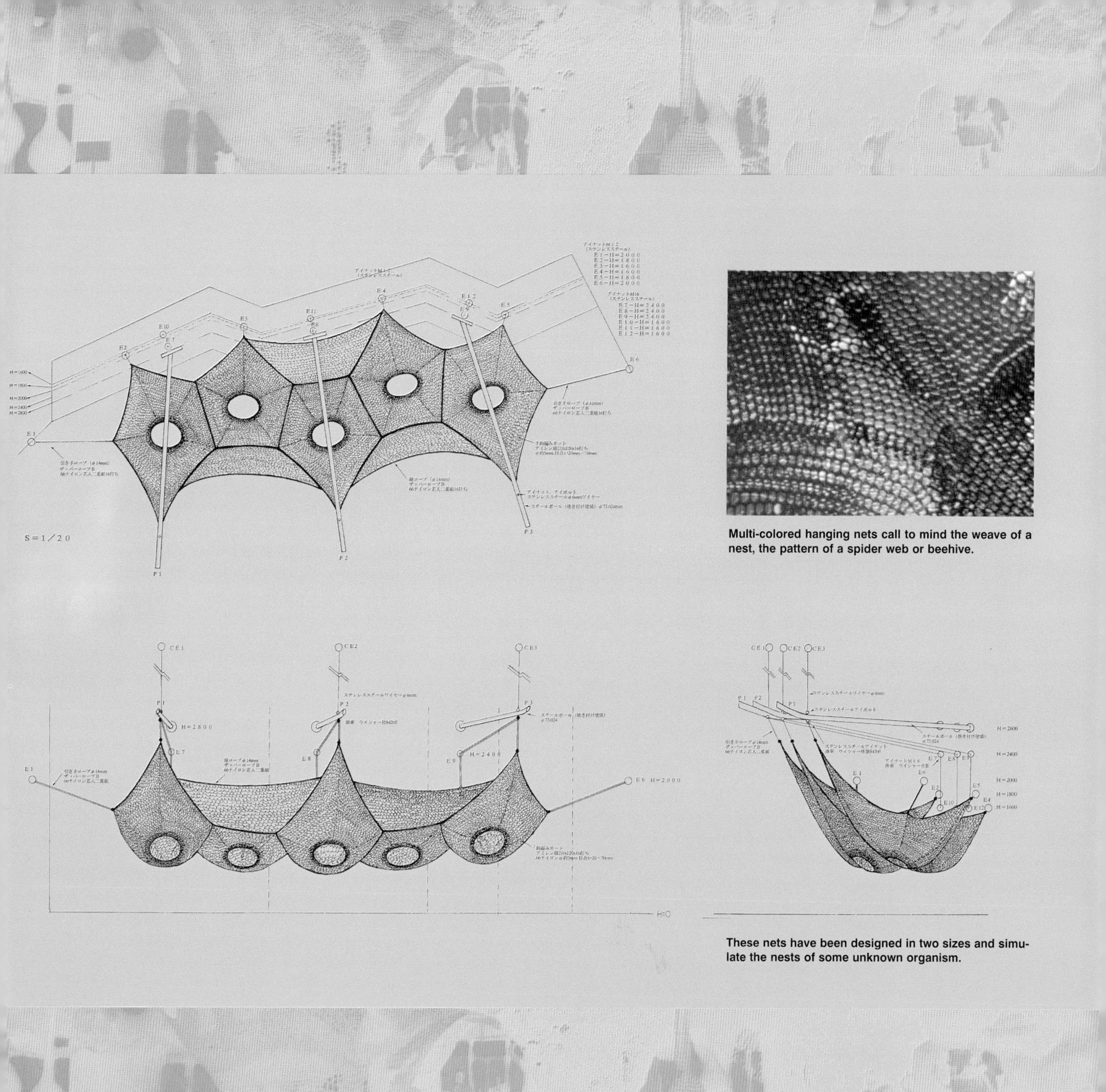

Multi-colored hanging nets call to mind the weave of a nest, the pattern of a spider web or beehive.

These nets have been designed in two sizes and simulate the nests of some unknown organism.

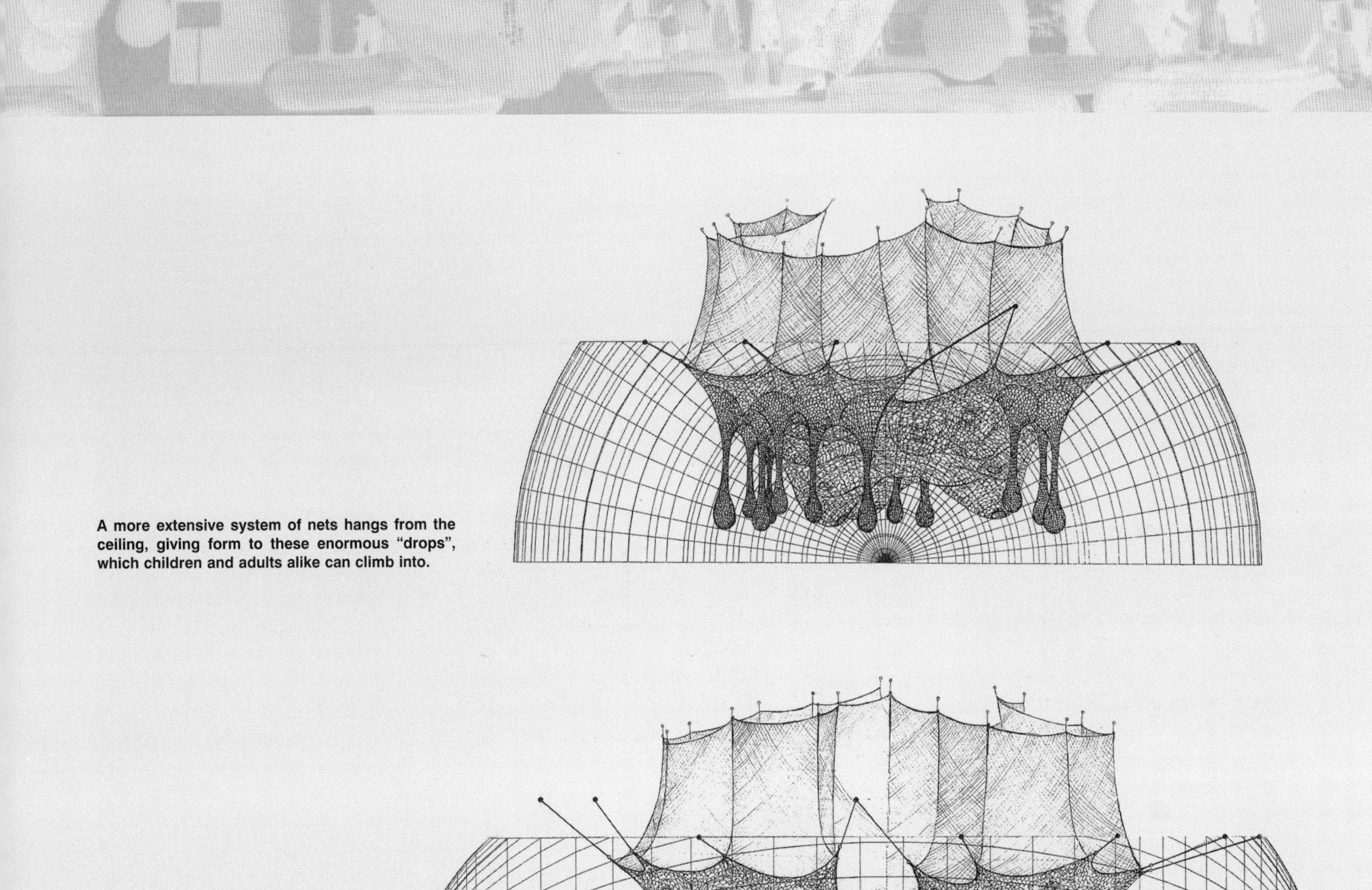

A more extensive system of nets hangs from the ceiling, giving form to these enormous "drops", which children and adults alike can climb into.

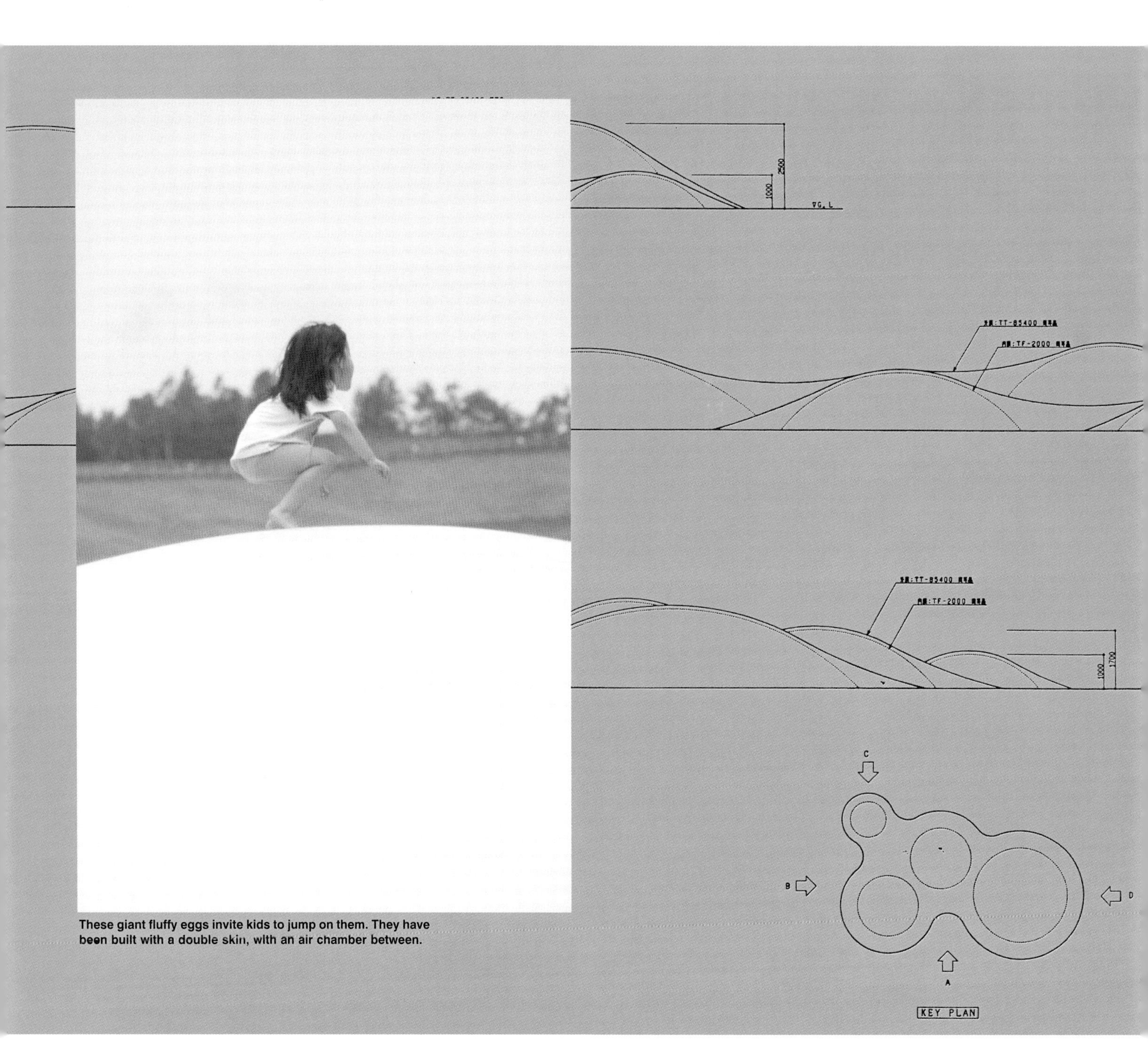

These giant fluffy eggs invite kids to jump on them. They have been built with a double skin, with an air chamber between.

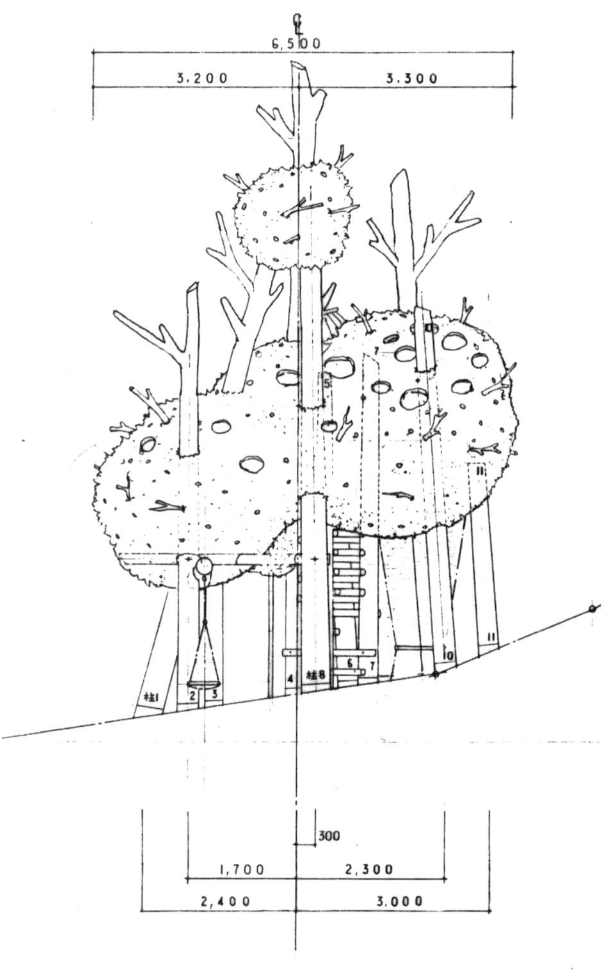

A giant bird's nest includes insulation to help visitors understand how such constructions work in nature.

Taylor Cullity Lethlean

photographs: Carla Gottgens, Ben Wrigley

Carlton Gardens

Playground

Melbourne, Australia

The brief for the Carlton Playground required the designers to reconcile two competing objectives; to provide a contemporary playground space that would be at once rich in play opportunities and respectful toward its historic parkland setting. Whilst the Carlton Playground is designed for children and their parents, its sculptural aspects have also been designed to be complimentary to the adjacent Museum.

On one level the design is loosely based on a traditional labyrinth or maze. A series of linear walled forms in pre-cast concrete are dissected with paths and punctured with openings here and there, providing a variety of running, hiding and exploratory experiences. One serpentine shape is sequentially repeated, with each succeeding position being slightly shifted, lowered or raised. The resulting linear voids between the walls almost seem to be excavated from the landscape. This is an intentional contrast with its impression from the adjacent street or the museum, where the play space undertakes a richly colored and visually dynamic experience. The design of the playground has won awards on two occasions from the Australian Institute of Landscape Architects (AILA).

The basic design is a maze formed by a series of linear pre-cast concrete forms, which are square in plan and intersected by the playground's main paths. Two sophisticated, industrial-looking play structures have been placed within the walls of the maze as if they had sprouted directly from the adjacent museum.

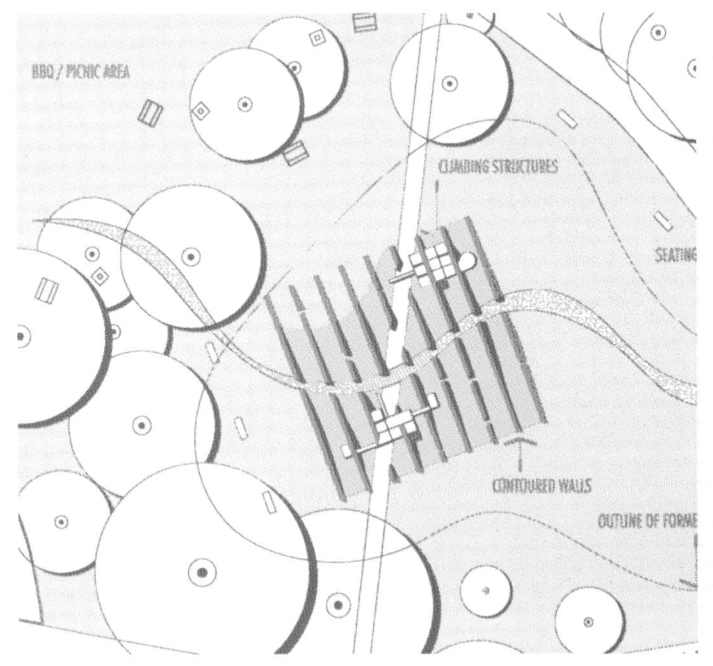

Viewed from within the Carlton Gardens, the play space is visually integrated into the landscape. The maze nestles comfortably into the site, with the walls being profiled to follow the topography.

Two metallic play structures stand out against the black and red waves of the walls. They are simple forms with attachments for sliding, climbing, hanging, tunneling and balancing activities.

The placement of these unique walls, which are perforated in places, suggests a wide spectrum of play activities.

MELB RNE USEUM

The park's sculptural forms provide a great diversity of changing perspectives and confer a dynamic look onto the play space.

Griendpark

Maastrich, Holland

Bureau B+B Photographs contributed by the architects

Two seemingly conflicting needs had to met in the design of the skate park in the Griendpark. On one hand was the desire to offer local kids a place to meet up with friends, skate and socialize. On the other was the need to create an aesthetically appropriate space that the general public could also enjoy. The ingenious end result deliberately emulates the look of ice floes floating on a blue northern sea.

The concrete forms (or, aesthetically-speaking: the "ice floes") are of such a height and shape that skaters can spend endless hours experimenting with them. The soothing blue background (the "sea") makes the skating area an attractive addition to the park.

The perimeter of the skate zone features painted markings resembling those on a helicopter landing pad.

Die Welle (The Wave)

Villach, Austria

Karin Zeitlhuber
/Reinhard Bernsteiner

Photographs: Mag.art.Reinhard Bernsteiner

The primary goal of this project was to create something truly new on the concrete surface that made up the leisure area of a trade school built in the 1960s. The designers' solution was a massive "fold", that is, the transformation of a two-dimensional surface into a three-dimensional space. This "wave" idea arose while bending and shaping a sheet of paper until achieving a ripple with one end touching the ground and the other forming an opening in the shape of a breaking wave. The end result looks something like a carpet with one corner pushed up.
It was very important that in turning the basic idea into a reality none of the design aspects be compromised for technical reasons. The final result should deviate as little as possible from the original design.
The body of the wave divides the space and modifies the visual references, while also comprising a large extension to the school, with various applications and a great deal of style.

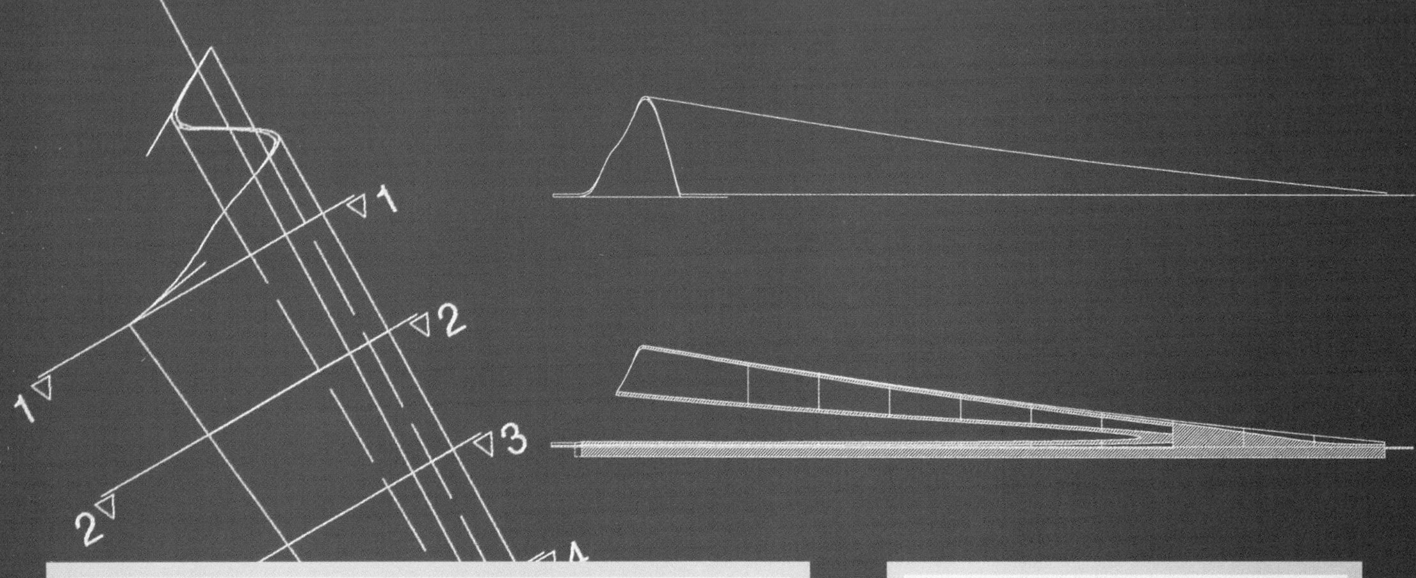

In order to establish a determining mathematical model, a specialized computer program was developed that, with the introduction of certain variables, allowed the designers to come as close as possible to their original paper fold.
The final technical aspects of the design were elaborated on the basis of the numerical determination of the wave. All of the surface points in the space were established during this phase.

The fold and the horizontal surfaces of the wave provide ample seating and climbing space, while the flat surfaces feature an integrated lighting system.

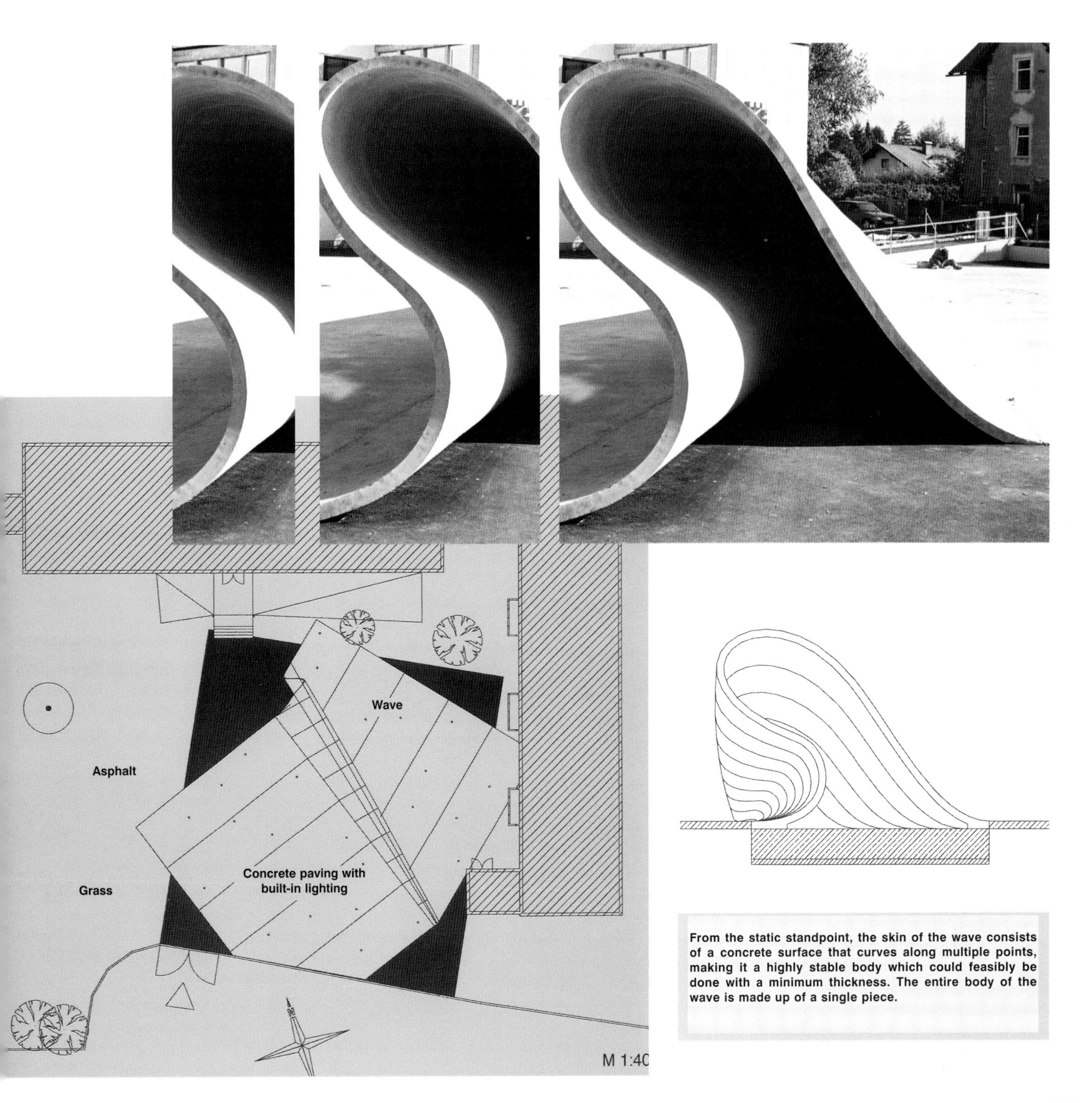

From the static standpoint, the skin of the wave consists of a concrete surface that curves along multiple points, making it a highly stable body which could feasibly be done with a minimum thickness. The entire body of the wave is made up of a single piece.

Büro Kiefer

Photographs contributed by the architects

Flämingstrasse

Berlin, Germany

play area and parking lot

Ordinarily built and designed under the sole criteria of cost effectiveness, parking lots are usually gray spaces devoid of all aesthetic considerations. They are the urban landscape's eyesores, relegated to secondary planning processes that seek to hide, silence or, at best, disguise them behind a thick barrier of plants.

The Büro Kiefer team, in collaboration with the landscape architect Martin Rein-Cano, has turned this notion on its head, converting what would have been an asphalted surface into a colorful playground for local children.

A ground surface painted electric blue forms the backdrop to a design which makes use of the language of street signs, although here for very different purposes. Large numbered signs fill the central area, which is adorned with bright splashes of red and yellow and a thick white boundary line. The idea is ingenious: a parking lot that neither denies nor hides its character while being worked into the cityscape and creating a fresh, invigorating "place" in its own right.

This peculiar parking lot sits at the foot of the Marzahn building (known for its low energy consumption) to the east of Berlin.

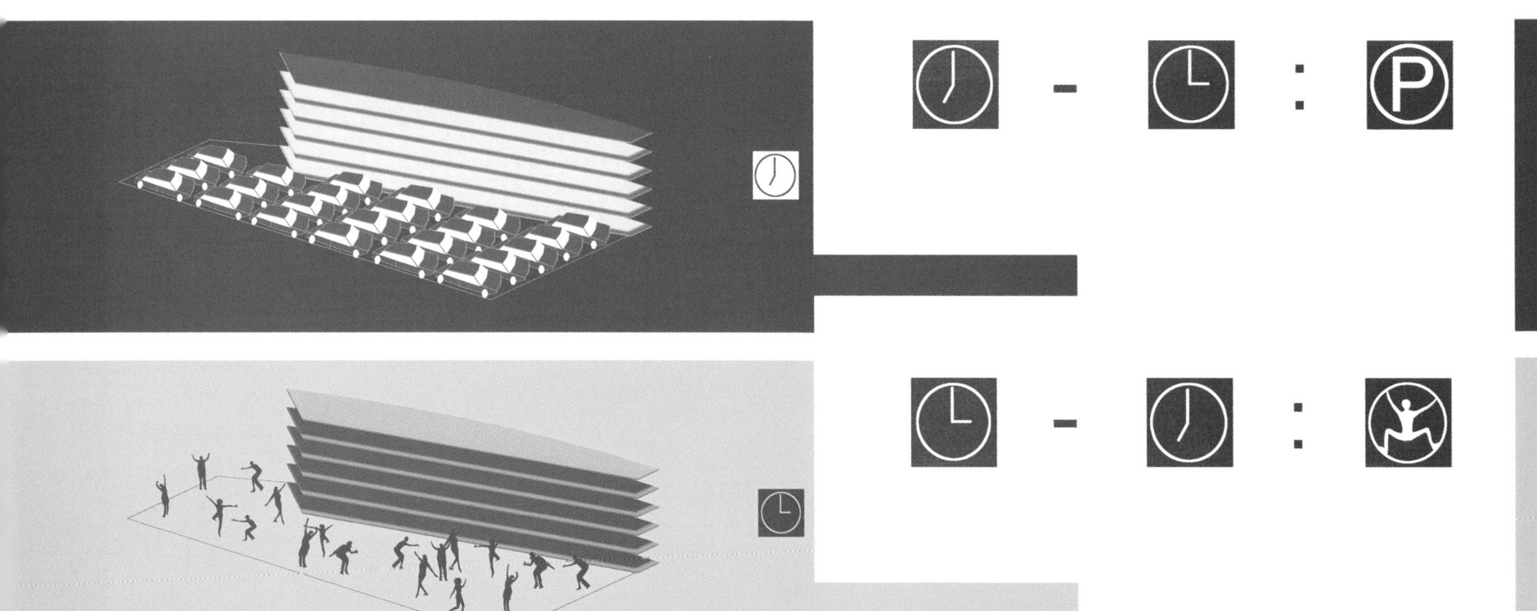

Established hours dictate when the space shall be used as a parking lot, and when the time has come for the children to use it as a playground.

Color is one of the determining components in this spectacular design.

16

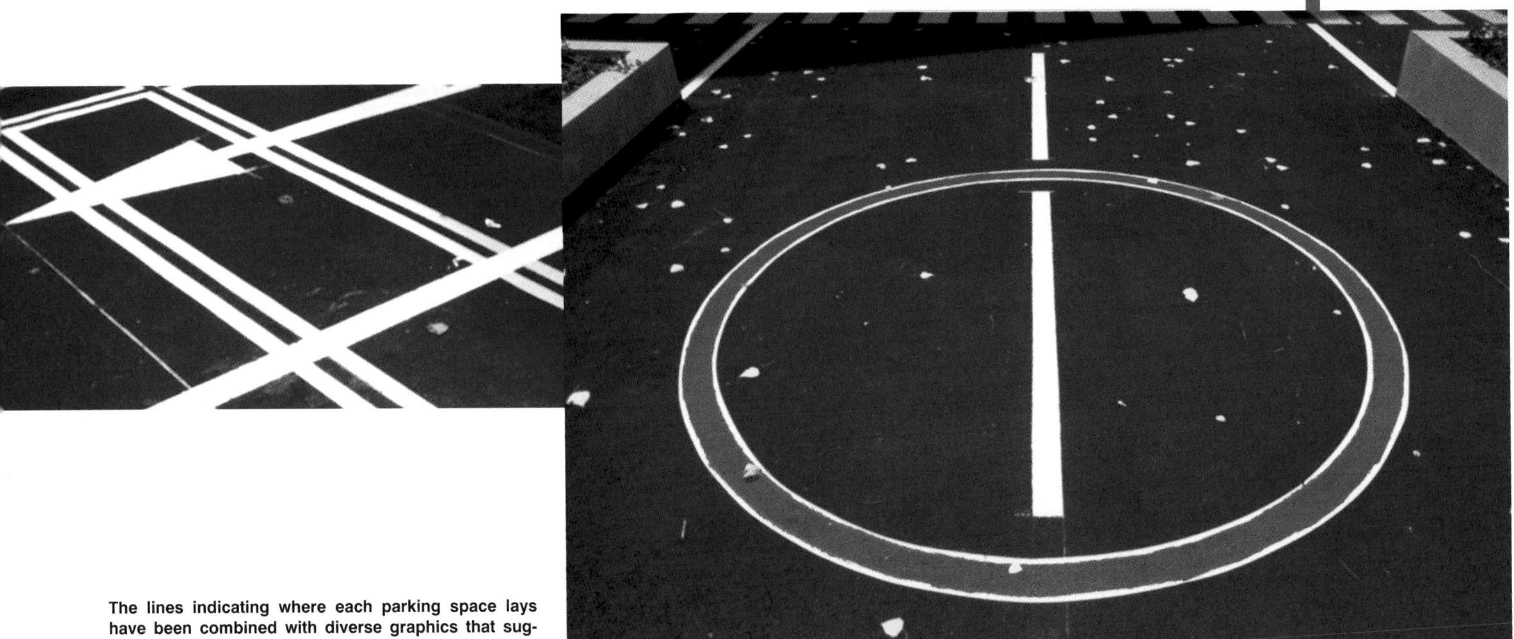

The lines indicating where each parking space lays have been combined with diverse graphics that suggest all kinds of games and activities.

2

In combining such disparate needs as a parking lot and a playground, the design process has become a highly plastic experience culminating in the recuperation and recognition of a unique space for the city.

Kijo Rokkaku

photographs contributed by the designers

Tokyo, Japan

Shiru-ku Road

We are increasingly dependent on visual perception, with print media, on-line material and the visual imagery of television and movies dominating our attention at the expense of the other four senses. However, attempts have been made to escape from the emphasis on the visual and to restore sensitivity to the capacities of touch, smell, hearing and taste.
The Oasis Project for Suginami district in Tokyo is one of the most promising of such experiments. Suginami district's urban design project is known as "Shiruku Road" (the first word is written with characters that mean "know your district", but the phonetics make a pun on the "Silk Route" through Asia).
It is centered on two large-scale circuit pathways linking the principal parks and public facilities of Suginami. Residents can extend their knowledge of the local environment by walking these paths, riding their bikes, playing, stopping at museums or just relaxing and enjoying the trees and flowers.

The Barefoot Oasis is designed to awaken tactile sensitivity, with visitors being led through a system of paths.

At periodic stopping points, a predefined sequence of body parts is addressed: forehead, arms, chest, stomach, fingertips and the soles of the feet.

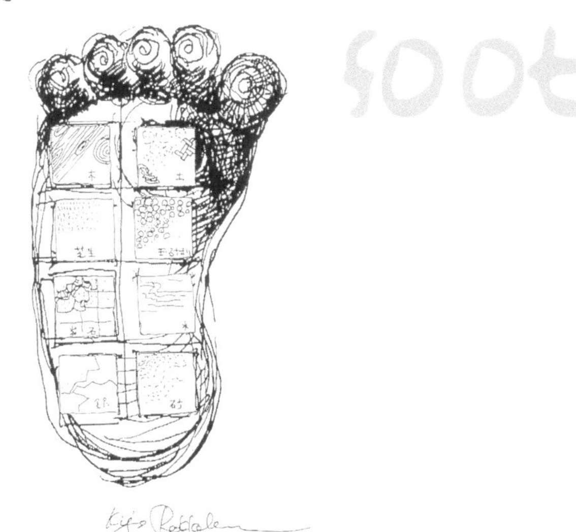

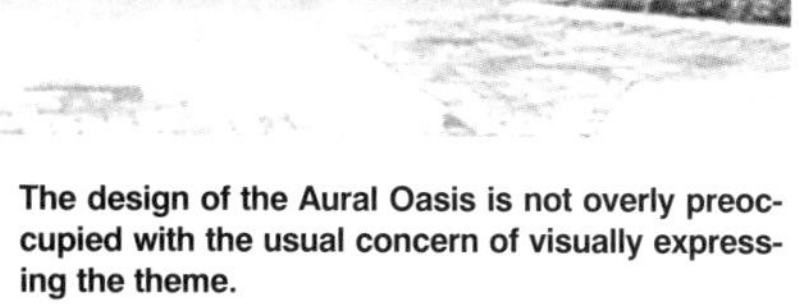

The design of the Aural Oasis is not overly preoccupied with the usual concern of visually expressing the theme.

Seven types of auditory device are provided to communicate both the whisper of the bamboo leaves and the resonance of the wind behind them.

This section of the park offers the opportunity for kids to stop and simply listen in peace and quiet, something they cannot always do surrounded by the noise and activity of the city.

smell

Even the sense of smell receives attention in the design of the park, with these metal chambers that capture and concentrate the scent of the foliage in the park.

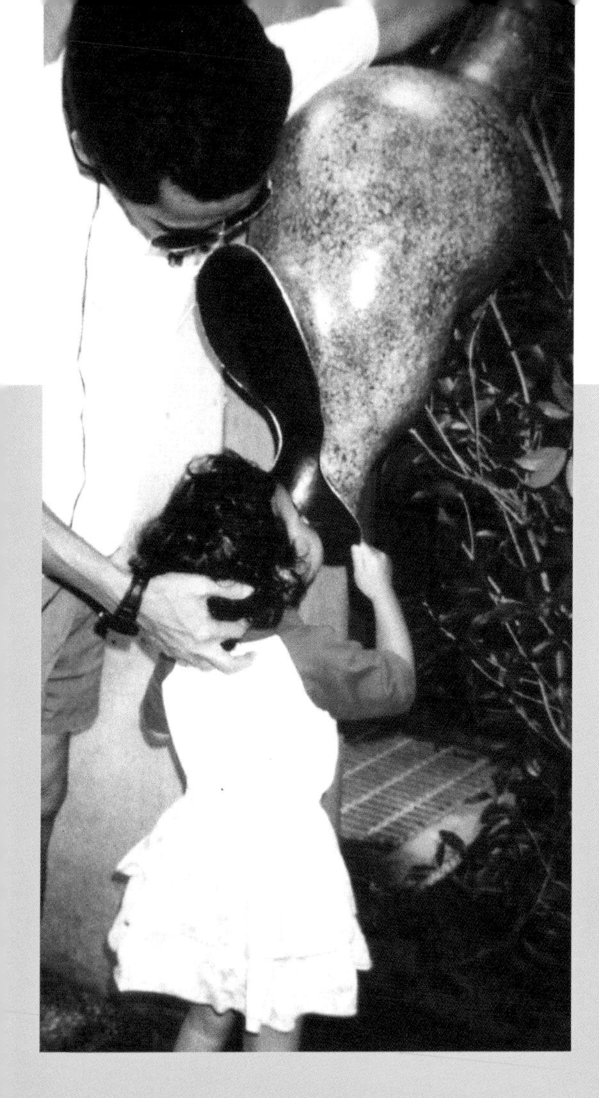

While we are constantly surrounded by changing odors, we are seldom aware of them. The design seeks to bring children's attention to this neglected sense.

The scents captured by these chambers vary throughout the year as flowers bud and bloom.

At the Time Oasis, moving parts have been kept to an absolute minimum, ensuring a restful atmosphere.

Valkenberg Park

Breda, Holland

Refined details and the addition of custom-designed fixtures have given this established park a fresher, more stylish aspect. This includes the large children's sandbox, designed in the shape of an oval terrazzo dish. The dish, measuring 18 x 12 meters, is the color of sand and lies slanted in the ground so that it is easy to climb into on one side.

Bureau B+B

photograph contributed by the designers

Reflexes

Girona, Spain

Martirià Figueras

photographs contributed by Martirià Figueras

This temporary installation in the patio of the Girona courthouse is a feast of sight sensations inspired by the shifting dance of light and reflections in the leaves of a forest. Figueras views it as an echo of paradise lost, an evocation of the Garden of Eden and, thus, of the primordial concept of the first garden.
This "forest" consists of nine metal trees with multi-colored plastic leaves that refract light, bouncing it off the watery surface below. This type of installation, which has been designed to provide enjoyment and encourage participation in all age groups, is especially fascinating for children as it bathes the space in specks of light, both through the air and on the water, making it an interesting addition to any playground.

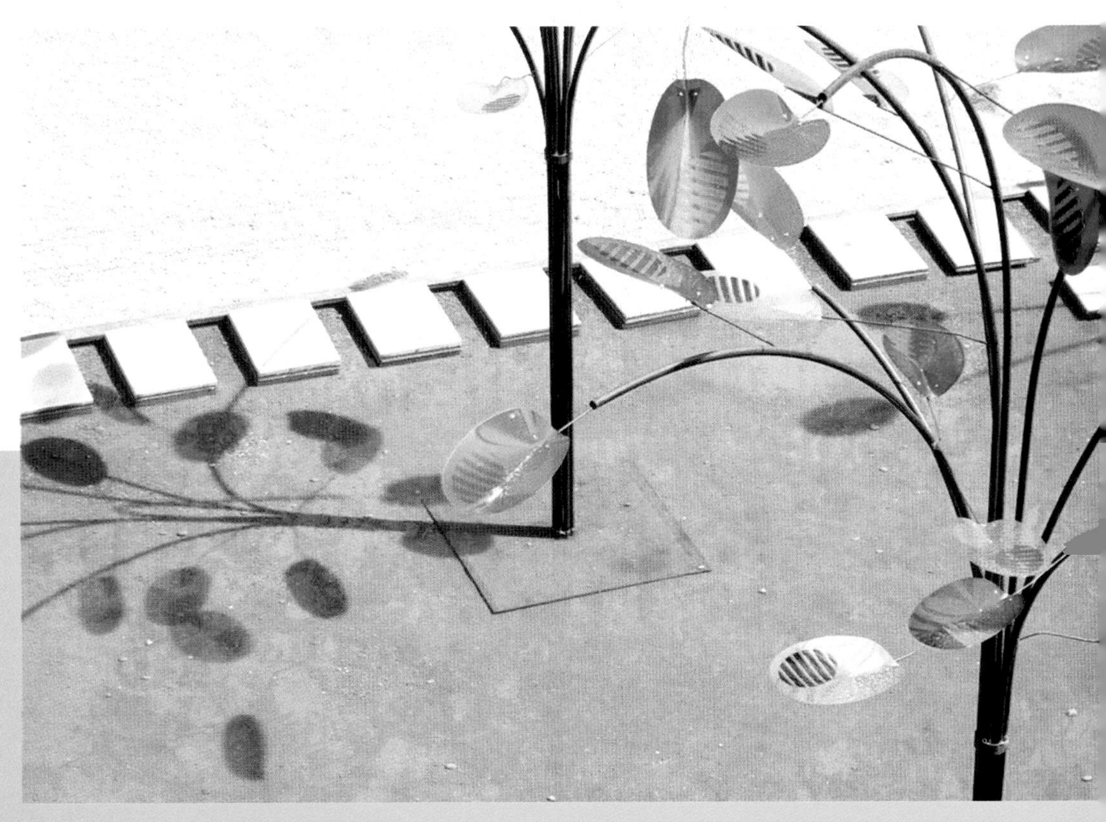

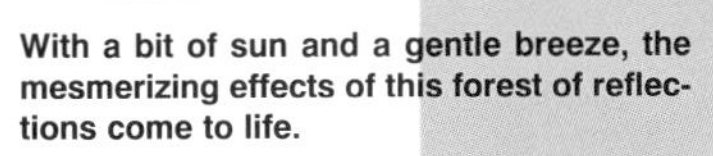

With a bit of sun and a gentle breeze, the mesmerizing effects of this forest of reflections come to life.

Specks of color are scattered across the sky and along the surface of the water, where sunlight is refracted, thus increasing its properties of relaxation.

Birken III

Marktheidenfeld, Germany

Robin Winogrond photographs: Kai Loges, Hans Fuchs

According to Robin Winogrond, catalogue play equipment comes with 2 general problems. It is virtually impossible to integrate into its urban context, making it look something like a landed UFO. Furthermore, toys are replaced as quickly as children's interests and abilities develop, whereas a child playing at the same kindergarten for 4 years is confronted with the same slide, swing and sand year after year regardless of his or her developmental stage. Therefore, in the program for the Birken III Kindergarden Playground, Winogrond decided to do away with conventional play equipment and instead provided unique elements which would be open to multiple uses.
In Birken III, large sculptural play elements have been designed to stimulate the imagination; they act in a capacity similar to a theatrical set design which gives clues to the content of the play, yet here the story is completed by the authors: the children who make use of the equipment. The pedagogical principle that children respond to contrasting experiences such as high/low, alone/in groups, hiding/being the center of attention, physically active/mentally active was also used. The entire space can be read as an enormous plaything with over a dozen ways to ascend and descend the terraces.

Birken III is like a miniature landscape. What is seen in each of the shapes depends on the dose of imagination at work.

y of space and imagination: birken III
nogrond, 1994/1995

his playground responds to and is integrated i
t, the entire site treated as a single
large sculp

objects/landscapes act as catalysts for imagination to
project their own reality onto the objects, so
set designs which give clues to a stor
interprete it in his or her own way.

a new kindergarden buildin
remain at the kindergarden for

the building an
vastly different forms. one of the ma
and integrate the two forms, at th
clear form to the garden itself. the cen
is echoed in the earthforms, concret
of trees. the topography, which fell d
to create a small plaza for group pla

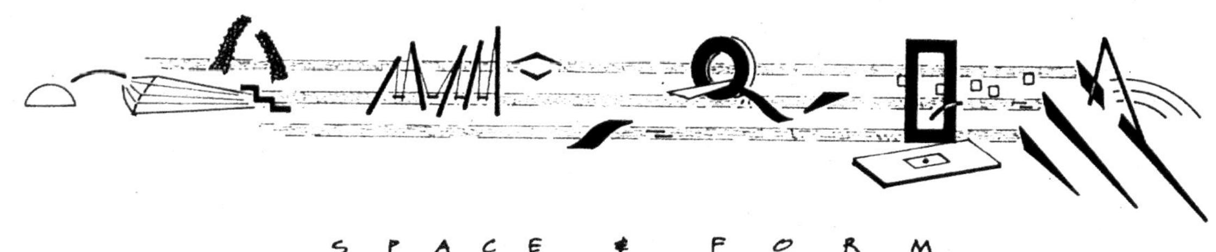

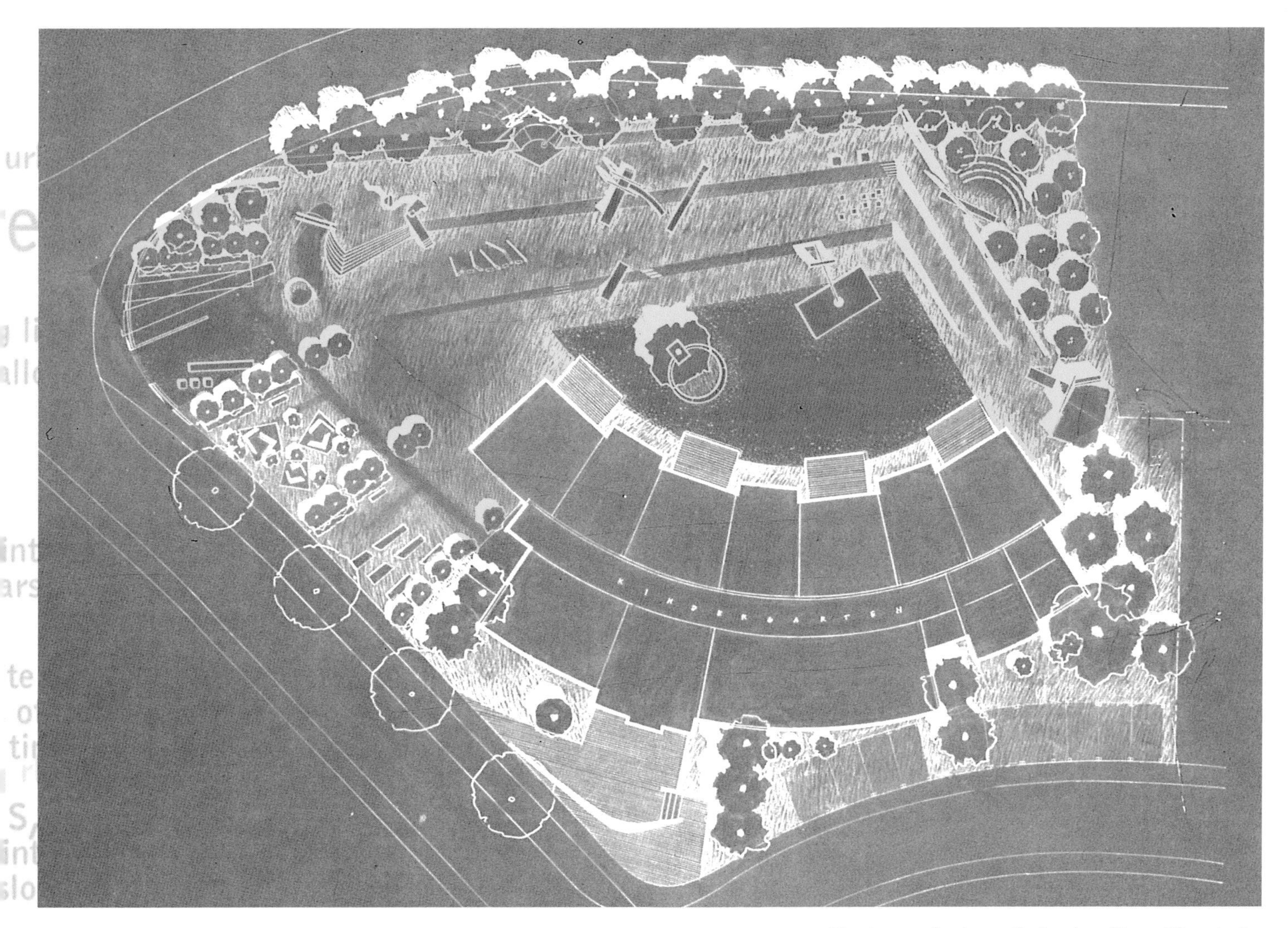

The playground embraces the fan-shaped form of the school.

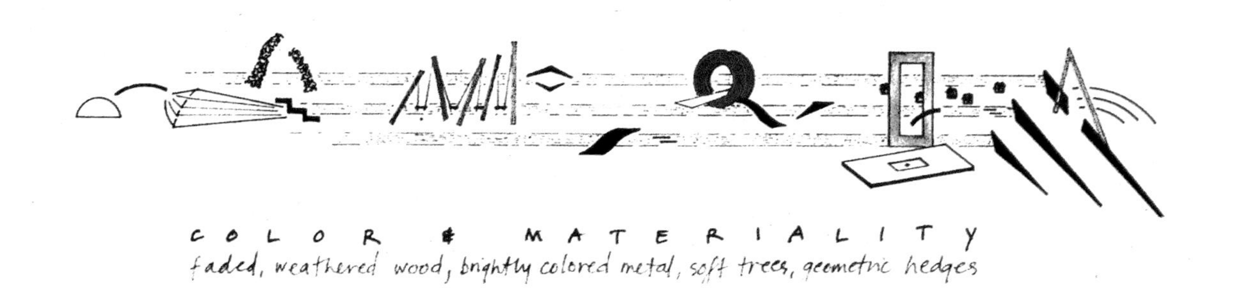

The huge red O offers a perfect stage for showing off
and a nice ride down the slide.

These fun boxes, which come in different sizes and in varying degrees of transparency, beckon kids to play “hide and seek” or “house”.

These terraced slopes are another spatial stimulus in the playground.

A 3 x 5m raised, slate surface waiting to be drawn on in chalk. With the press of a button an arc of water shoots through the frame to wash away the drawings and begin again.

Nothing and everything is as it seems: these sculptural swings could very well be giant crayons nailed into the ground. And the door glimpsed at the top of the stairs just might give way to any number of surprises.

Photographs contributed by the architects

Beatrix Park

Almere, Holland

The skating area in Beatrix Park is itself a playground within the overall space. The skate park is a concrete landscape that encourages different forms of recreation. The design motif is simple: gently curving bowls dug out of the earth or mounds rising above ground level. The overall result is a constantly varying landscape which kids can really make the most of.
The surface of the 6000 square meters of concrete in the skating area was intentionally left bare from the start in order to encourage graffiti and drawings. The local youth, through this form of expression, help to anchor the skate park in its social context.

Bowls of varying depths and diameters fill the entire space.

The concrete of this artificial terrain forms gentle waves and curves, as if it were plastic.

ONLY

Not only do kids spend hours of enjoyment here roller-blading and skating, but they also find in this space an ideal atmosphere for socializing.

La montaña mágica

Barcelona, Spain

EMBT Arquitectes Associats SLP

Photographs: J. Krauel

At over 14 hectares, the Parque Diagonal Mar is one of Barcelona's largest parks. It forms part of the work done along the city's seaside zone in honor of the 2004 International Forum on Culture. This wide open space thus forms a link between city and sea, with constant references to the Mediterranean and its natural surroundings. The plant species chosen, for example, are either indigenous or have been adapted to the Mediterranean climate. Organic shapes abound, whether in the plants themselves or in the design of the benches and fixtures found throughout the park.
Designed by Enric Miralles and Benedetta Tagliabue, the park has a playground, a large lake, an area for sports, and countless original elements, such as the Magic Mountain, which is flanked by spectacular slides, designed by the architects themselves.

The silhouette of the slides recalls the gentle curves of the dunes gracing the coastal landscape.

Each of the four slides is of a different width and degree of slope, and culminates in a patch of sand.

The differing degrees of slope are adapted to accommodate different age groups, while the curves of the sliding portion keep kids from going too fast on the way down.

Pyramiden spielplatz

Ostfildern, Germany

KNÖLL OKOPLAN

Photographs: Andreas Peyker

This is a playground which is nonetheless devoid of elements that are specifically identified with play activities. Rather, the design is meant to incite the children's curiosity and abilities in getting a feel for their surroundings through spontaneous playing, open-ended situations and improvised adventures. Sculpted, grass-covered hills are perfect for exploring, climbing, sliding down, hiding behind - in short, they set an ideal stage for children to give their vitality free rein. Additional elements, such as slides, climbing walls and stepped levels, make use of the natural lay of the land. A stand of willows has been turned into a series of informal huts and a labyrinthine system of tunnels with narrow co-rridors spilling out into open spaces, all of which is perfect for playing hide-and-seek or for learning how to find one's way around.

designing a playground

Index

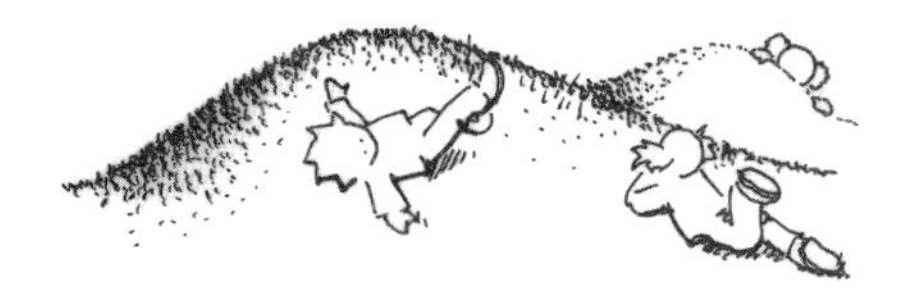

Designing a Playground 267

Growing
What are we going to play?

1. The Play Area 271

1.1 Interacting with the Surroundings
The lay of the land
Plants
Water
1.2 Differentiated Spaces and Uses
Inside and out
Everything in its place
1.3 Let's All go to the Park
No barriers
Accesses and routes
Side protection for paths
1.4 Up and Down
Steps and stairs
Ladders
Ramps
1.5 Paving
1.6 Take a Deep Breath

2. Playground Equipment 281

2.1 Things to Keep in Mind...
Materials
Handrails and railings
Boundaries
Supports
Joints, bolts, edges
3.2 Slipping and Sliding
Types of slide
Parts of the slide
Widths and surfaces
3.3 Swinging and Rocking
Types of swing sets
Parts of the swing
Distances and surfaces
3.4 Climbing
Climbing on rigid equipment
Climbing on flexible equipment
3.5 Composite Playground Equipment
3.6 Playing with Nothing - Shapes
3.7 Learning through the Senses
Sounds
Watch, see, observe
Touch and texture
...and smell!
3.8 Building - Playing with Sand and Mud
3.9 Splashing Around - Playing with Water
3.10 On Wheels

4. Ensuring Safe Play Conditions 295

4.1 Padding Impact
4.2 Minimum Space
The area of impact
Obstacle-free fall height
4.3 Protection Against Getting Stuck
Getting the head or neck stuck
Getting the extremities stuck

Designing a Playground

We have now seen how each designer's creativity and imagination are manifested in a thousand different ways and with exceptional results. Some of the play spaces and their components may seem elaborate, others less so. Even behind the seemingly simple designs lies a sense of experimentation and the will to provide good, fitting stimuli for children. Furthermore, the design of a recreational space must answer to this need, while taking into account a series of aspects that go beyond mere formal discourse.
This appendix deals with these topics in a structured and straightforward manner. There are three sections, which are preceded by an introduction reflecting on the activity of playing and on the different ways that children play. The first two sections comprise, respectively, a number of guidelines and suggestions for planning a playground, and the design of playground equipment. The third is a concise section dealing with safety issues from a design perspective.
In sum, this appendix complements the practical examples that we have already seen, providing a series of basic norms for drawing up the first sketches of a new playground or playground equipment and helping define the guidelines toward a definitive layout.

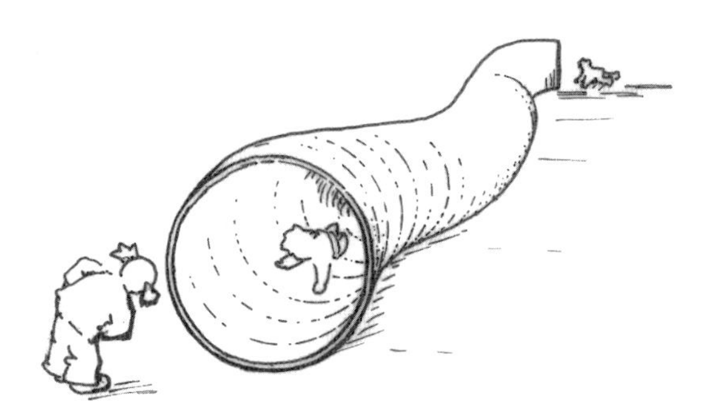

Growing

Children go through different stages marked by evolving ways of playing as they grow. While we need to understand these stages in order to create suitable play spaces for each age group, it is also important to remember that all children are different and that preferences and needs may vary among, and even within, each age group.

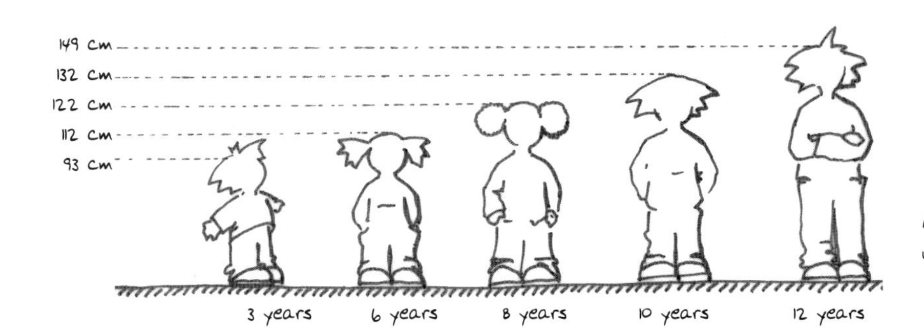

As we grow, the games that we enjoy also evolve.

Broadly speaking, we can establish the following growth stages, and the play habits observed in each phase:

0-3 years

Children acquire their formative experiences and learn to control their own movement in the first three years of their lives. They usually play alone and tend toward experimentation with touch, sight and sound. Playing in sand, clay, water, swings and slides (the last two with the help of an adult) are appropriate for this stage.

6-8 years

From age 6 to 8 children gravitate toward activities which involve movement and action; activities which develop both organizational and physical skills. Children in this age group enjoy testing their dexterity with elements such as climbing nets and other more or less complex structures that call upon different motor responses.

3-6 years

Between 3 and 6 years of age, and with the onset of social awareness, children usually play in groups, thereby fostering interpersonal relationships and sociability. Children in this age group enjoy activities which represent something else; for example, they play with abstract elements, tables, benches, as well as with swings, slides and movable equipment.

8-10 years, and upward

As adolescence nears, children opt for grouping together, but without adult supervision or interference from younger children. Structured games with objective rules played in groups or teams tend to predominate at this age. They also like to demonstrate their powers of balance and coordination in more complex climbing equipment.

What are we going to play?

Keeping active. Physical games.

Highly physical play activities, such as jumping, running, cycling, crawling, climbing or sliding often require nothing more than a good space equipped with adequate protection against bumps and falls. Nonetheless, it is always advisable to ensure some form of modular play equipment, structures and varied terrain, all of which provides a range of possibilities for interaction and dynamic games.

The traditional game of "tag", a type of physical game.

Getting along. Social games.

Social or relational games are those that involve chasing, hiding and role-playing in groups; imagination is the primary tool used in such activities. Since only very basic means are required to stimulate the imagination, it is more effective to provide abstract, suggestive elements which the children will adapt in their own way.

Hide-and-seek: social games do not require complicated elements.

Imagining. Creative games.

Material which can be molded or transformed such as sand, grass, water, gravel or clay is used in this type of play. It's hard for a child to keep still when presented with these materials; the physical properties of such elements enable children to develop a wide variety of activities in which the imagination and creativity are of prime importance - qualities of which the smallest children are true masters!

Here comes the train! (Anything is possible when you're playing in mud!)

Experimenting. Sensorial games.

Although the senses are involved in all human activity, children are the true pioneers in experimenting with them, which is why those play elements that necessarily involve sensorial experience are especially recommendable. In addition to elements designed for stimulating the sense of touch, auditory, visual and even olfactory stimuli can be incorporated.

Channeled sound.

...and playing in peace and quiet

Providing opportunities for rest and reflection in a playground is just as important as encouraging physical activity. A child's choice to play alone, quietly, should therefore be respected. In order to create the appropriate environment for achieving this, one or various spaces should be set aside and shielded from the noise and activity of the other play areas. In so doing, we provide a setting where children can concentrate on their activity free from outside interference or distractions. At the same time, we gain a peaceful spot that adults can also enjoy. Here, we can set up sand boxes, tables and benches and also ensure that the area is adequately protected from excessive exposure to the sun.

Playing peacefully in the sand.

1. The Play Area

Before beginning the design of a play area, it's a good idea to pay a visit to a playground that is already in use. There, we can observe the children's reactions to certain spaces and play equipment and take note of how each situation unfolds. Children can be the harshest of judges in their own way, which is why a positive response to a certain playground arrangement or element is a highly gratifying experience for the designer of that space.

For example, kids enjoy variety in their playground equipment and spaces; that is, the opportunity to play any number of games or activities. When something doesn't bring about the desired result, they get bored and quickly throw themselves into something else. To avoid boredom, the play equipment should be attractive and suitable for each age group and for different levels of activity. It should also provide diverse stimuli for promoting a child's development - equipment designed to encourage social skills, integration with others and respect for the environment. It doesn't take much to achieve this; no matter how limited the available ground space may be nor how restricted the budget, it is important to never underestimate the possibilities of a future playground. Excellent play opportunities can be provided with even the minimum of effort and resources.

The freedom to design, however, must be subject to regulations for making sure the equipment is safe for its users. Everything in a children's park or playground must comply with each region's specific technical norms concerning playground equipment. The safety precepts and dimensional requisites on the following pages, unless otherwise stated, correspond to the European standards on playground equipment (1176:1998), published by the European Committee for Standardization.

The following information should not be taken as a substitution for local norms. It is herein included in order to provide some useful guidelines for the professional designer as well as the layperson. These basic recommendations will be of use in drawing up an outline for the future playground, play equipment or even a private backyard, safe in the knowledge that the spaces for our children are being looked after in a creative and responsible way.

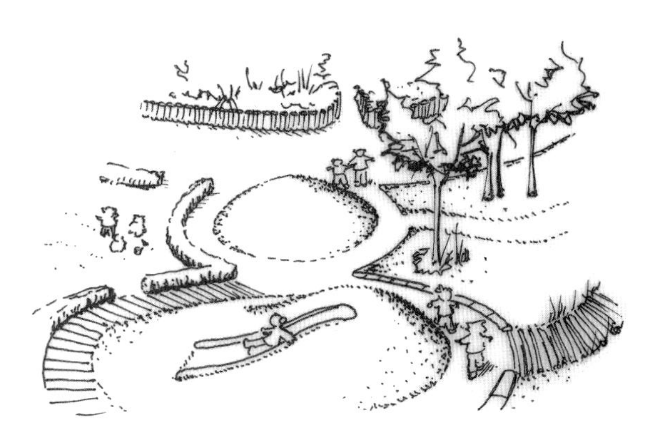

1.1 Interacting with the Surroundings

The lay of the land

The first conditioning factor in any future playground is the configuration of the ground surface where it is going to be placed. If the occasion (and privilege) of being able to work on natural terrain arises, we can greatly enhance and simplify the design of the playground if we respect the existing topography.
Since children respond more enthusiastically to irregular forms than to uniform, rectilinear shapes, the possibilities of a natural area in and of itself for providing ample play opportunities are considerable indeed.

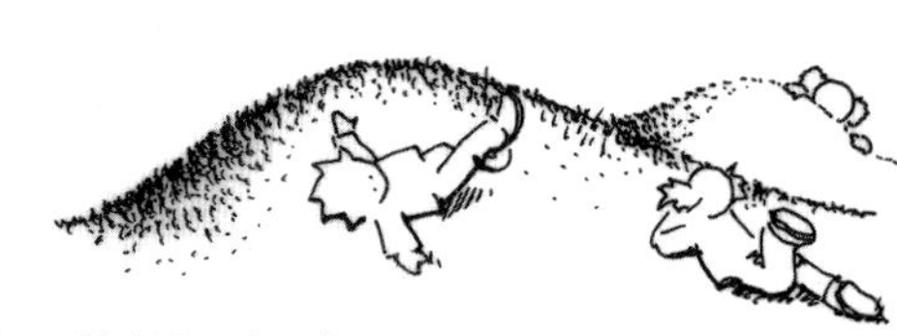

Playing with the rise and fall of the land.

Lengthened, curvilinear forms are preferable over squares and lines.

We can, for example, experiment with the anomalies of the terrain, making use of changes in level, accentuating or softening slopes and setting up different zones at different heights. Children enjoy imagining adventures, "getting lost" and finding their bearings, rolling down the slopes, playing hide-and-seek with the rise and fall of the land or "king of the mountain".
In any event, even if the site offers few opportunities from the start, we can always add the design of hills, slopes, caves and a variety of other elements that provide good stimuli for playing, while also encouraging children to explore the environment and hone their spatial abilities. With such simple touches as these, the results couldn't be better!

Vegetation

Vegetation is a highly valuable element in the design of any space intended for use by children, whether for its environmental or aesthetic aspects, or simply for fun.
Plants improve air quality and serve as a protective barrier against rain and sun, both on their own or in conjunction with pergolas or similar structures. Additionally, dense plant species mitigate wind and reduce noise - or at least alter sounds by generating their own. And, of course, plants are a natural habitat for birds and other small animals, making it a prime consideration to conserve and protect any existing vegetated area there may be on the site.
In any event, bringing in new plant and tree species can contribute to the creation of a unique environment that will enhance the educational properties of the activities to take place in the

Tall plants and trees mitigate the effects of the sun and rain.

park. For example, if we plant deciduous plant species, sunlight will penetrate the canopy in the wintertime, while plenty of shade will be ensured for the summer months. Also, with fruit trees, children receive firsthand knowledge of seasonal life cycles.
It is especially important to conserve and incorporate any existing trees into the project, unless they present a danger to the health of the children. Mature tees offer an appealing, solid aspect which saplings and recently-planted trees have not yet acquired. Furthermore, their placement might lay the groundwork for the layout of a design that will undoubtedly reflect sensitivity and respect for the environment, invaluable qualities in any project these days.

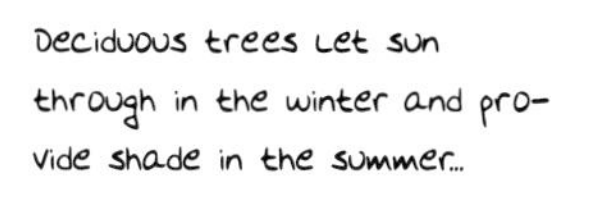

... and fruit trees provide firsthand experience of the life cycles of plants.

Playground activities can be very harmful to the vegetation, especially to shrubs and other low-lying plant species. Thus, wherever new plants are added, resistant species appropriate to the environment with a high capacity for regeneration should be chosen.
Before deciding upon a given species, it is important to know if the park is going to receive sufficient care at regular intervals. Untended vegetation may mar the overall look of any playground as well as involve risks for the children. This does not mean that, faced with the prospect of scarce upkeep, we should have to do without plants. On the contrary, there are numerous species that do not require special attention and that produce excellent results.

Water

Children particularly enjoy water, even more so when they are allowed to touch it or play in it, as we will see in section 2.9.
Any existing natural water should be conserved and worked into the project as far as possible. Highly valuable ecosystems depend on creeks, canals, ponds, swamps and natural springs; the project should work around and respect them. These water habitats will also encourage children to observe and learn about life cycles and the natural environment.

Aquatic ecosystems are a valuable source of learning about the natural environment.

1.2 Differentiated Spaces and Uses

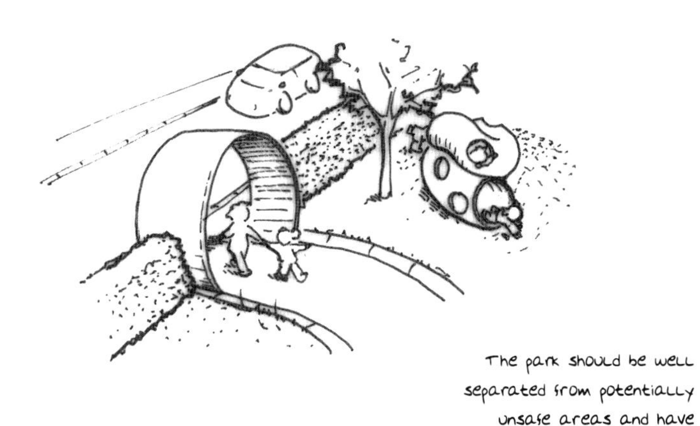

The park should be well separated from potentially unsafe areas and have clearly marked accesses.

Inside and out

For obvious safety reasons, the borders of a playground should be well defined. Areas where safety conditions cannot be controlled, such as surrounding roads, must be physically separated. These delimitations can be achieved with natural elements, such as shrubs, for example, or using artificial solutions, such as walls and fences.

Bearing in mind how children love to scamper up and over objects in a playground, care should be taken to avoid making these peripheral structures look climbable. Their height and surface treatment should be such that kids are not tempted to climb, sit or stand on them. Additionally, it is important to clearly identify the park's entrances and exits and to make them easy to access from primary roads and circulation routes.

Everything in its place

Ensuring a certain degree of organization in a playground is a necessary aspect so that children learn to find themselves within a space and get their bearings among different play areas.

A prior classification of the activities that are to take place in the playground is a good place to start; it will help establish spatial relationships according to criteria of function and use. For example, we will differentiate the zones intended for group activities and those where children can play individually: noisy, physical activities should be kept apart from the area set aside for quieter games. This area, in turn, could be placed in relation to the areas of the park set aside for rest and contemplation or at the outer limits of the site.

Very different or incompatible activities should be appropriately separated.

The playground should be sheltered from the wind.

Borders between different or incompatible play areas should also be easily recognizable, whether they be physical, visual or acoustic markers. Although these areas should be differentiated and independent, they should nonetheless be somehow linked so as to encourage relations between different groups.

A few more details to keep in mind: whatever layout chosen in the end, we should consider whether the play areas, especially those for the smallest children, can be easily seen from other points of the park. It is also recommendable to set up sunny and shady areas, places sheltered from the wind and rain, all according to the climate and necessities of each geographic zone.

1.3 Let's All Go to the Park

In order to create a fertile environment for social interaction, we should include spaces that encourage children to play together.

Above all, a good design must be based on the idea that all children are different and therefore may have very different needs. All children should find equal opportunities for entertainment and recreation in a playground; to meet this goal, we should come up with play spaces that allow them to interact and learn together.
We should pay special attention to the smallest children and those with mental or physical limitations, these being groups for whom play time is especially important.

No barriers

Up until only a few years ago, playground design, as with many urban projects, did not take into account the fact that many visitors may have difficulties in freely moving about in the established spaces. Fortunately, public spaces are now designed to be accessible to the handicapped; each geographic zone has its own accessibility regulations to meet this end.
Ensuring a barrier-free space involves more than simply leaving out equipment or objects that may obstruct the use of a space; it also means that we should consider incorporating specific elements - without making excessive alterations or compromising the design - that can be enjoyed by all visitors.

The smallest children and those with some sort of handicap need special attention.

Keeping everyone in mind: for example, a raised planter helps protect plants while also allowing all users to reach it.

Alternatives to steps (a ramp, for example) should be included on all playground equipment.

Accesses and routes

Paying particular attention to accesses and routes in a playground is fundamental for ensuring equality of conditions for all children. For example, if stairs and slopes are complemented with ramps, we resolve one of the most frequent problems of accessibility for persons with reduced mobility. If it is not possible to make the route flat, slopes should be moderated to less than 5% and include corresponding resting spots at regular intervals, given that moving along inclined surfaces is especially tiring for users with motor difficulties.

It is advisable to route various types of paths through the playground, each one diverging from the main path so that children can feely explore. These itineraries can overlap, split apart and provide alternative routes while at the same time enriching the design of the park. Narrow paths and cul-de-sacs should be avoided in all cases, as they are trouble spots where children might collide. We can also set up circuits for tricycles and bikes that are sufficiently differentiated from the footpaths in order to avoid possible collisions.

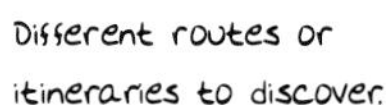
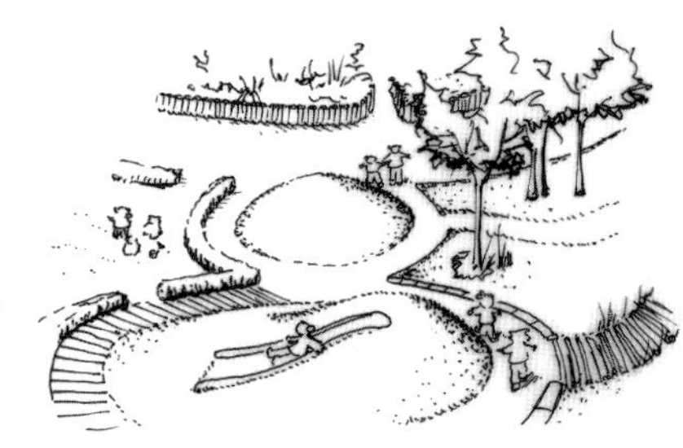

Different routes or itineraries to discover.

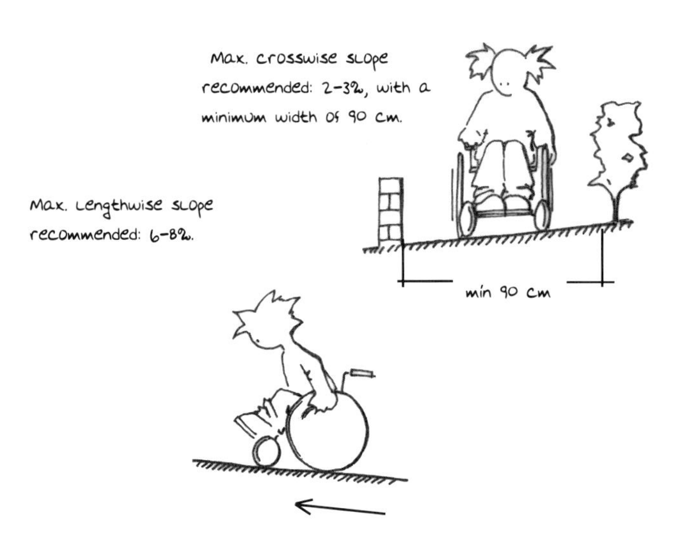

Following accessibility criteria, a route, installation or space might be:
- Adapted, if it meets all of the necessary functional and dimensional conditions to be used comfortably by persons with impaired mobility or sensory abilities.
- Practicable, if it meets the minimum conditions to be used by persons with reduced mobility or sensory abilities.
- Convertible, when it can become practicable or adapted through simple, low-cost modifications.

Itineraries	Adapted	Practicable	Convertible
Width	90-180 cm	90-120 cm	90 cm
Maximum lenthwise slope (for ramps)	6-8%	8-10%	10-12%
Maximum crosswise slope	2%	3%	5%

Side protection for paths

Steep slopes or inclines where falls are more likely should be protected by handrails or curbs. Sidewalks, for example, should be included in tight spots or in areas where it may be hard to get through; and an identifiable change in material should mark practicable itineraries for people with poor eyesight.
The need for fixtures such as paved sidewalks, curbs and handrails is dictated by the degree of accessibility at any given point and by the particularities of the site and of contiguous vertical levels, in which case it is also necessary to check local accessibility regulations. Most regulations also state that branches, leaning tree trunks and other vertical elements might be dangerous if they overhang or otherwise interfere with footpaths; therefore, none of these elements should be within the range of the footpath at a height below 2.10 meters.

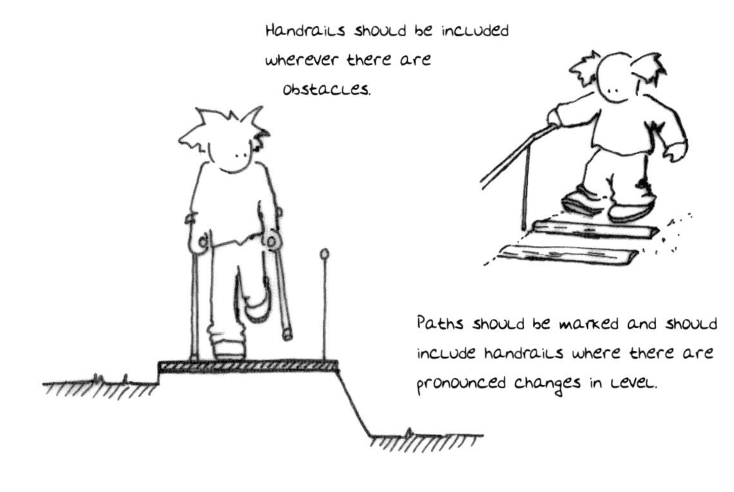

1.4 Up and Down

Steps and stairs

Contrary to appearances, stairs are often more comfortable than ramps for people with impaired mobility. We should therefore pay special attention to this aspect of the design, adhering to regulations regarding accessibility in public spaces.

Adapted stairs should have handrails on both sides.

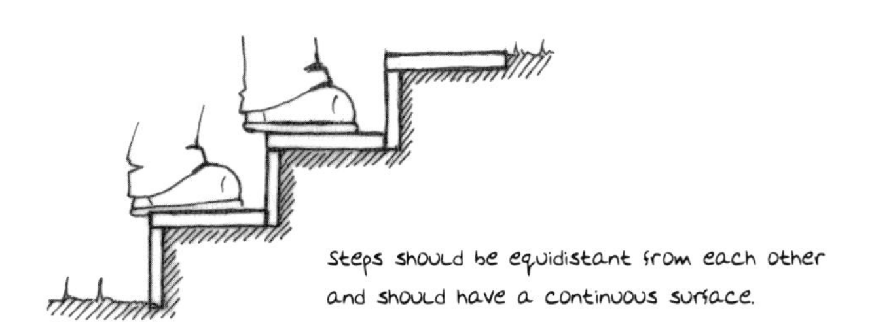

Steps should be equidistant from each other and should have a continuous surface.

Steps and stairs on play equipment are different from conventional steps and stairs in that they must comply with a unique set of requisites dictating size and safety. Summing up the characteristics common to both types of access, stairs should have a constant inclination with equidistant steps and should be of uniform construction. Especially long stairs should be divided, with platforms placed at intermediate intervals.
The upper surface should be covered with some sort of non-slip material to avoid slips and falls. Additionally, handrails should be placed on both sides of adapted stairs in order to ensure that all users can get a good grasp on it.

Ladders

Ladders are used primarily for enabling access to the uppermost point of a structure or playground equipment. The most common ladders are generally those providing access to slides and modular equipment with platforms at varying heights. Being inclined, ladders occupy very little surface area, a characteristic which makes them appropriate for most playground equipment, which is usually on a smaller scale to accommodate the youngest children.

The crossbars and steps of a ladder should be placed at equidistant intervals.

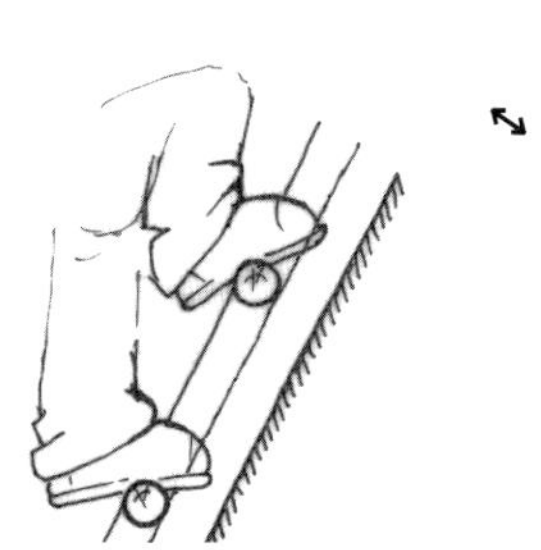

The space above each crossbar should allow for sufficient foot support.

As opposed to standard ladders, their use requires foot and hand support, although a handrail will do if necessary. Crossbars and steps should therefore have adequate, unobstructed space for foot- and hand-holds and should be equidistant and stationary.
Wherever possible, playground equipment should include alternative access routes (as opposed to conventional ladders) so that children with motor impairments can use it without difficulty.

Ramps

Getting around on sloped surfaces can be especially tiring for users with impaired mobility: a ramp which is too long or with an inadequate slope can render a path useless for those who really need it. Therefore, we should pay special attention to the length and maximum degree of inclination of the ramps to make them comfortable to use and effective.

Bearing in mind the physical effort involved in getting around for people with motor impairments, it is important to keep the minimum distance between the ladder and its ramp alternative.

The ramp should have a non-slip surface.

A ramp broken up into shorter sections is preferable over a long, continuous ramp.

We should also remember that not just any sloped surface will function as a ramp. Technically, a ramp is a surface with a slope of between 5% and 10%, and up to 12% in extreme cases. The degree of the slope should be constant along the entire length and, in the event that the ramp has to be especially long, it should be broken up into shorter sections which are separated by level platforms at each turn. The handrails or walls should begin at the lowermost point and the surface should be non-slip.

The specific details for the correct dimensions of the ramps are also included in the regulations governing such structures in each geographic zone.

1.5 Paving

Depending on the necessities and characteristics of the location, various types of surface treatments are used in playgrounds. Thus, a footpath requires a paving material different from that used in the swings and slide area, where there is a consistently higher risk of falls. (Section 3.1 contains information on material for padding falls.)

In general, all paving in a playground should be stable, firm, able to pad falls, with a texture that is not too rough and a non-slip surface in both wet and dry conditions. Naturally, any joints or discontinuities in the paving should be treated so as to not obstruct movement in a wheelchair or on crutches.

Paving should be stable and have a non-slip surface.

Different combinations of textures and colors in paving in order to achieve a specific effect -whether for informative or purely aesthetic reasons- can be highly inspiring for kids. This can be done where we wish to provide information, mark a change in direction or a transition from one play area to another, to distinguish areas for rest and relaxation, and so forth. Additionally, changes in texture can be detected by blind children and even particularly bright colors can be perceived by visually impaired persons.

1.6 Take a Deep Breath

Areas for resting

A space, no matter how small, where a child can sit quietly and relax or gather strength to continue playing is an invaluable addition to any playground.

In larger playgrounds, it is a good idea to create rest zones at regular intervals. Such zones must comply with the corresponding accessibility criteria. European standards recommend that in adapted itineraries the distance between these zones should range between 45 and 60 meters; and in practicable itineraries, this distance should not exceed 200 meters.

A rest zone might be composed simply of a set of benches or other seating elements that are protected from the wind and rain. An open area equivalent to a circle of one and half meters in diameter should be set alongside the benches in order to allow wheelchair users to maneuver without difficulty.

Finally, the rest zone should not be set in some leftover, fringe area, since another essential function of such a zone is to encourage children to socialize with others. They should therefore be located near play areas that display different characteristics and that are intended for different age groups.

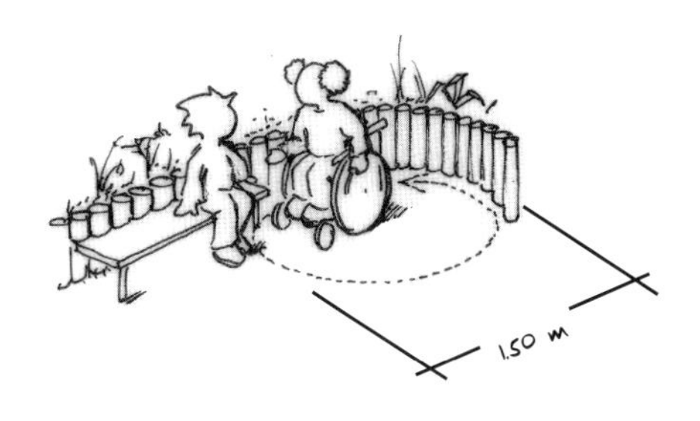

Space for wheelchairs set alongside the benches.

A rest zone to encourage social interaction.

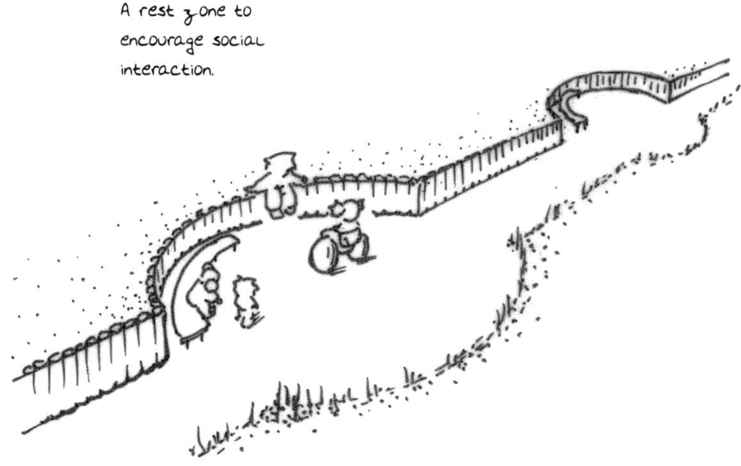

2. Playground Equipment

Although there is a seeming infinity of standardized playground equipment on the market, designers often prefer to create their own pieces, custom-tailoring them to a specific playground and its peculiarities. These one-off pieces come to define the playground's distinct character. Most of the projects featured in this book use exclusive playground equipment in their design - equipment which may or may not be combined with more conventional structures.

Building play equipment does not just involve coming up with an attractive and fun design, but rather calls for ensuring that the finished product is completely safe for children. The choice of basic material as well as surface finishes and the addition of elements to safeguard against falls are all equally as important, making it often more comfortable and preferable to rely on professionals specializing in the field of playground design.

Numerous companies and playground equipment manufacturers specializing in highly creative and innovative playground equipment have sprung up in recent years. These new designs show a clear tendency toward interactivity in an effort to integrate educational functions with the playground's more obvious reason for being: fun. Thus, sound-producing elements or games with water, for example, are now frequently worked into the design of play areas.

Classic playground equipment, such as slides and swings, are still widely used; in fact, they have never gone out of style and are included alongside custom-designed pieces in most newly constructed playgrounds. While swings have undergone scarce formal variations, a certain evolution can be seen in the design of slides, in material as well as shape, the overall end-goal being to make them both more innovative and safer.

However, in contrast to the newer and more or less sophisticated equipment, there are always those tried and true elements which do not depend on the availability of a large budget: the classic sand box is a good example, or simple wide open spaces for running and playing. After all, it's the imagination that counts.

2.1 Things to Keep in Mind...

Materials

Materials which facilitate durability, hygiene and ease of maintenance should be opted for when constructing playground equipment.
To begin with, neither potentially toxic elements nor raw metals (which rust or may act as conduits for electricity) should be used. Metal should be painted, galvanized or otherwise treated to prevent rust. Wood is a good alternative to metal - it should be of a kind that

Materials should be non-toxic.

Wood should not crack or splinter.

does not splinter and, in any event, should be thoroughly treated (meaning more than a simple surface work-over) to avoid splinters or irregularities that can snag or cut. If synthetic materials are chosen, they must also be durable enough to avoid splintering and cracking. The treatment of surface finishes, especially on rough or uneven material, is another basic consideration in greatly reducing the risk of injury. (See section 3.3).

Handrails and railings

Handrails and railings are the most common safety elements in playground equipment. Handrails and railings serve not only as protection against falls, but they can also be gripped and used as support and stability. They should therefore be designed for an easy grip, according to the size requirements of the corresponding regulation.

Railings protect against falls.

Handrails should be easy to get a hold on.

The height and diameter of such lateral protection are established according to their placement - whether on ladders, ramps, walkways or raised platforms - and must comply with accessibility requirements for the area or equipment. The European standard stipulates that handrails and railings be placed at a height between 60 and 85 centimeters from the platform, ladder or ramp; recommended width and diameter of handrails is between 25 and 32 millimeters.

Boundaries

Whether or not boundaries are needed depends on the age group which will be using the equipment and also on the height of support surface to which the children will climb.
As with railings, boundaries also prevent falls from raised platforms, while also keeping children from climbing to certain heights. The design of the boundary, therefore, should be such that it does not encourage climbing, standing or sitting on it.

Barriers also keep children from reaching certain heights.

Barriers starting at 60 centimeters in height above the play surface are appropriate for play equipment for toddlers.

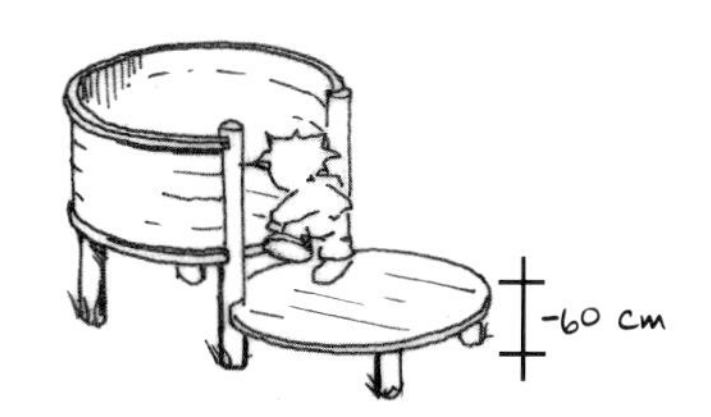

The boundary should completely enclose the perimeter of the raised surface, with the logical exception of the portion intended for entering and exiting the platform. If there are openings, they should be smaller than the size of a small child in order to prevent them from slipping through or getting stuck in the gaps. Boundaries should have a minimum height of 70 cm. from the surface of the platform, ladder or ramp.

Supports

Many play elements feature supports - which work indiscriminately for both hands and feet - for gripping, stabilizing or climbing. An effective handgrip should be of a size and placement so as to allow children to get their hand completely around it. It should be securely affixed to the main structure so that it will not come off or turn. According to the EU standard for an effective handgrip, it should be no wider than 60 millimeters, with a cross section of between 16 and 45 millimeters in order to be securely gripped. (It is recommended that those measuring 16 millimeters not be of wood, as such a thin piece may break.)

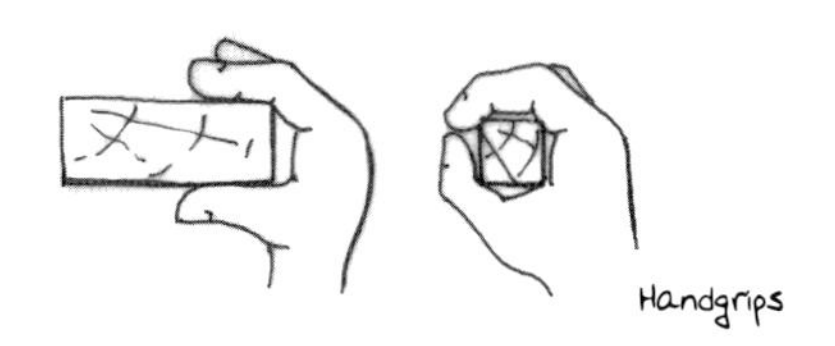

Handgrips

Joints, bolts, edges

Potentially dangerous protrusions should be protected.

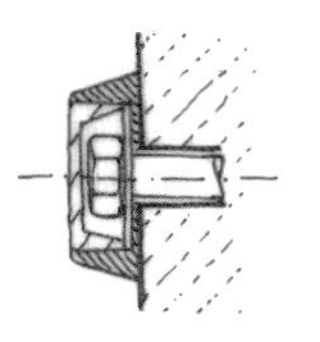

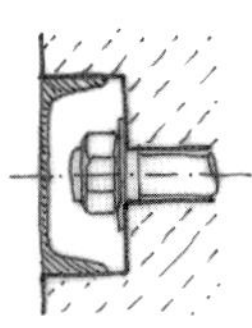

This category encompasses the outer edges of a piece of play equipment, as well as the system for affixing each of its components. As a safety precaution, sharp edges, pointy shapes and dangerous angles should all be avoided. Welded pieces should have smooth surfaces, and anything that anchors or holds the structure in place should be solid and stable. Nails should lie flush with the main structure, bolts should be covered by plastic caps and screws should not protrude more than 8 mm.

2.2 Slipping and Sliding

Kids have always been drawn to any type of inclined surface down which they can slip and slide, which is why slides are such a popular feature in a playground. It is rare indeed the playground that doesn't have a slide. Although there are an endless number of models on the market, it is often more appropriate to custom design a slide for a specific playground, whether the particularities of the site call for it, or whether it fits in with the general theme of the project or simply because we have the means to do so. No matter how valid a particular design may appear to be, bear in mind that it may not be apt for children; there are certain considerations of safety and size, according to the corresponding regulations, that must be adhered to. Here are some helpful general considerations:

Types of slide

Few pieces of playground equipment are available in such a variety of shapes and models as the slide. Their very nature is open to an endless number of options, from the standard freestanding slide with a ladder to the most complex models, which feature curves (even helicoids) and waves.

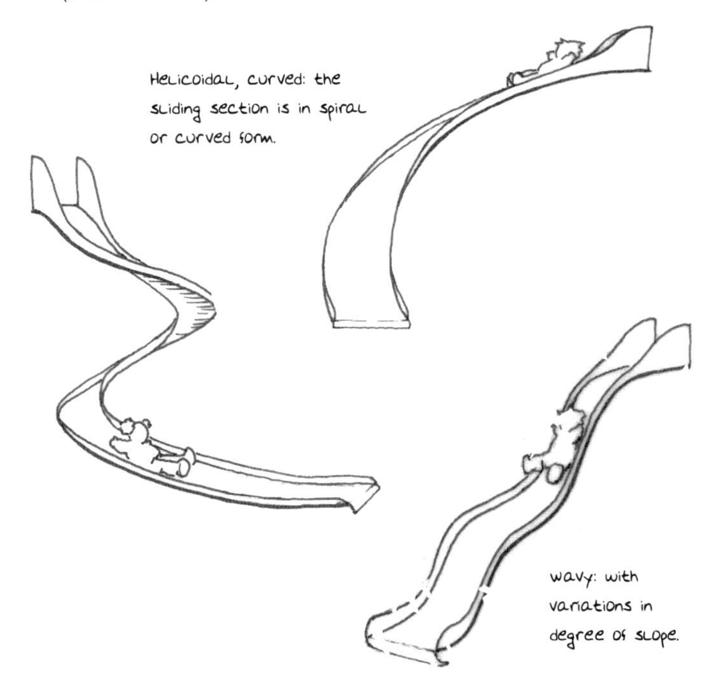

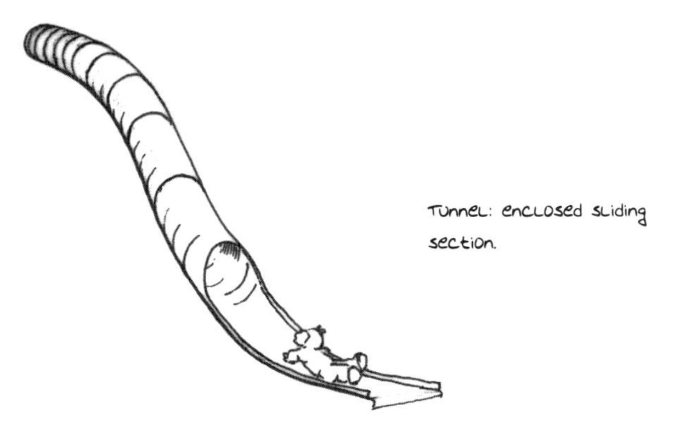

While most are open, it is becoming more common to find slides that are partially or entirely enclosed: tunnel slides.

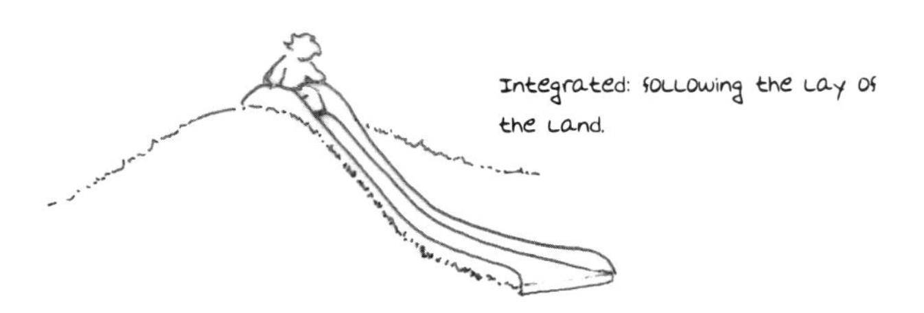

Terrain permitting, a good option is to integrate the slide into the lay of the land, thus achieving a more accessible solution for children with motor difficulties. This type of slide is one of the most visually attractive, each one becoming a unique piece in its own right.

Parts of the slide

No aspect of the shape of a slide is merely coincidental, but rather responds to series of requisites that make it safe and effective; not just any sloped surface can be considered a slide. Basically, this apparatus is made up of three parts: the starting point, the main section (the "slide" itself) and the finishing point. Each of these components slopes to a differing degree.
The starting point should be the same width as the main section and the transition from one section to the next should be smooth and continuous. It should be long enough to allow a child to comfortably and easily reach it and sit down.

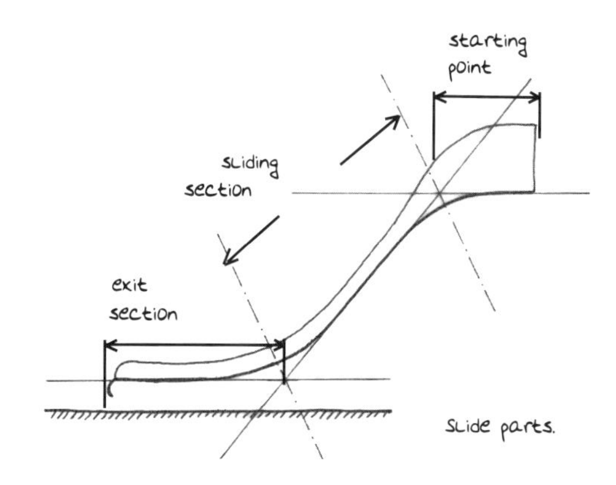

Slide parts.

All slides must feature an "exit" (the finishing point) in order to help the child maintain balance, decrease the possibility of possible crashes and make it easier for the child to get off the equipment. All finishes should be rounded or curved in order to avoid cuts and other minor injuries. The tunnel section of covered slides should be continuous until the final "sliding" portion, without including the exit point, which should be open as well.
Side protection is another highly important feature of the slide. It fulfills the dual function of ensuring that the child does not fall off and providing hand support. This feature can be perpendicular, curved or angled; the corners should be continuous and rounded in order to avoid cuts and other accidents.

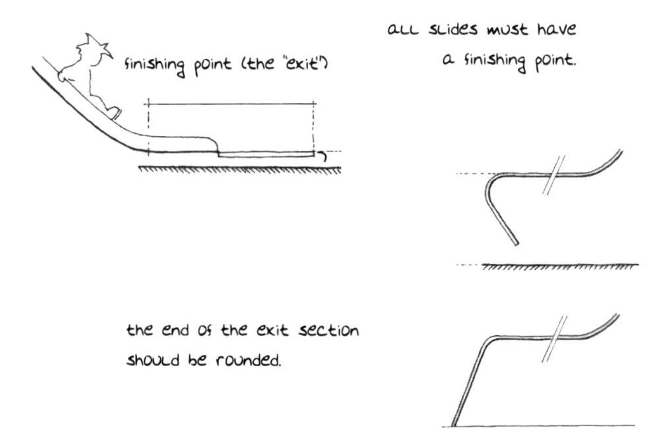

Widths and surfaces

The standard straight, open slide with a sliding section longer than one and a half meters should have a width measuring either less than 70 centimeters, or more than 95 centimeters. These dimensions ensure than children do not get stuck on the way down or tumble over on their sides, possibly getting hurt.
In curved or spiral slides, the width of the sliding section should be less than 70 centimeters. The minimum width and height of the interior of a tunnel slide should be 75 centimeters (the height being measured perpendicularly from the surface of the sliding section.
As all of the elements of a slide should avoid discontinuities that might snag clothing or where fingers can get stuck, it is highly recommended that the surface of the sliding section be of one piece. Metal slides should be installed in the shade so as to avoid possible burns caused by excessive sunlight heating the surface.

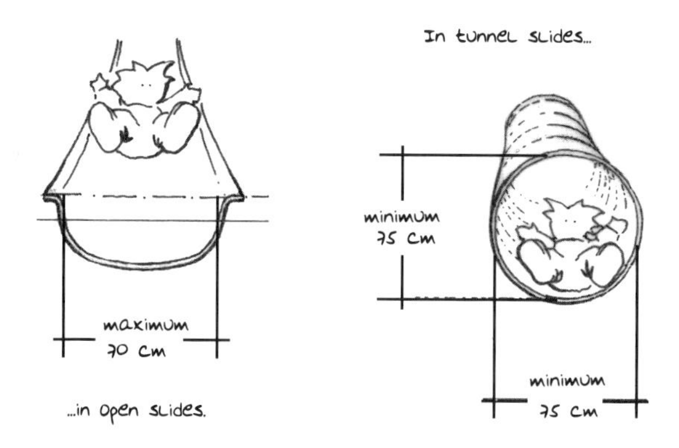

2.3 Swinging and Rocking

Swing sets, as with the slide, have become classics in playground equipment. The rocking of a swing has a calming effect, most notably with small children; it also helps develop the faculties of balance and coordination. Again, as with the slide, if we choose to custom design a swing set for a specific playground we must follow the technical specifications guiding the construction of playground equipment. Following are a few general design considerations.

Types of swing sets

A general primary classification of swing types is how many points of suspension they feature, one or various.
Swings with more that one suspension point are those with one or more axes of rotation. A swing with one axis of rotation produces a rocking motion perpendicular to the load bearing bar. Those with various axes of rotation enable a rocking motion perpendicular or parallel to the bar; in this case, the seat may hang from one or more bars. As a safety measure, it is not advisable to include this type of swing in conjunction with other equipment in a set.
Among the swings with a single point of suspension are the well-known classics using a tire; although there are now safer alternatives that are designed to look like tires and come in varying sizes.

Swings with a single point of suspension allow for multiple uses.

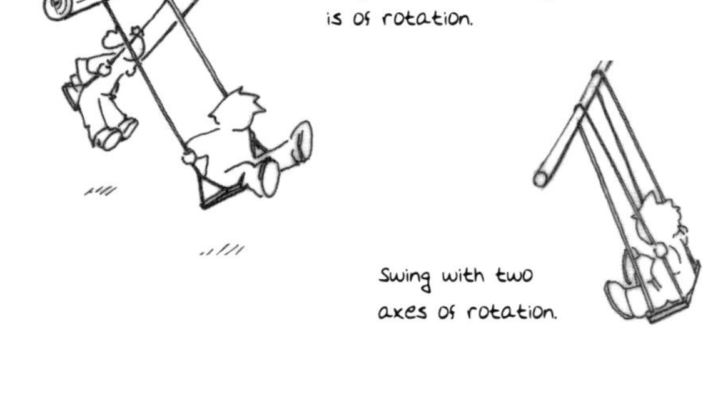

Swing with two points of suspension and a single axis of rotation.

Swing with two axes of rotation.

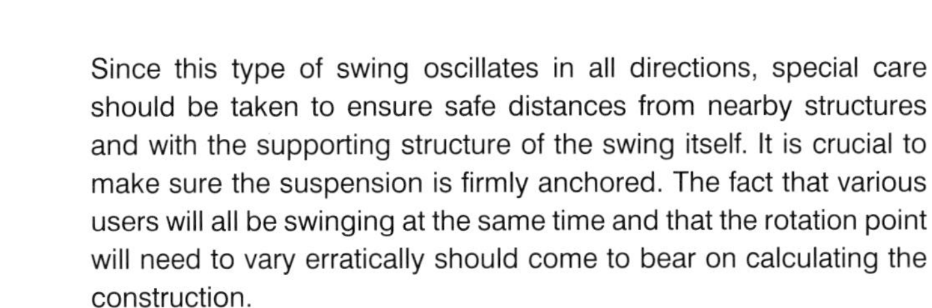

Since this type of swing oscillates in all directions, special care should be taken to ensure safe distances from nearby structures and with the supporting structure of the swing itself. It is crucial to make sure the suspension is firmly anchored. The fact that various users will all be swinging at the same time and that the rotation point will need to vary erratically should come to bear on calculating the construction.

Parts of the swing

A seat and the elements from which it hangs, in turn fastened to one or more load bearing bars and a structure anchored to the ground are the basic components of a swing.
The seat should be designed to hold just one user at a time. There are two broad groups of seat: flat, with neither back support nor side guards, and the so-called "harness" type, which provides

The seats on a swing set should permit only one user at a time.

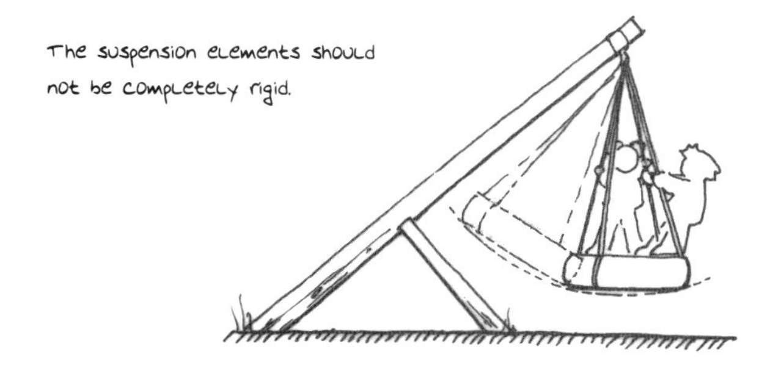

greater support for the smallest users or those with motor impairments. Materials with even a minimum degree of pliability should be chosen for the seats. Metal and wood are not recommended, as they could cause serious injury in the event of a child being bumped or hit by the seat.
Swings with one point of suspension can have platforms or tires intended to be used while standing. The material from which the seat hangs should not, in any event, be completely rigid. Chains and ropes are the most common solution used.

Distances and surfaces

More than two swings should not hang from a single load bearing bar in order to minimize the possibility of collision when the swings are in motion. Nor should we place two harness swings for small children alongside flat swings, which are intended for bigger kids. The minimum space between seats and between a seat and an adjacent structure in order to keep them from colliding or becoming entwined vary according to different standardized regulations.

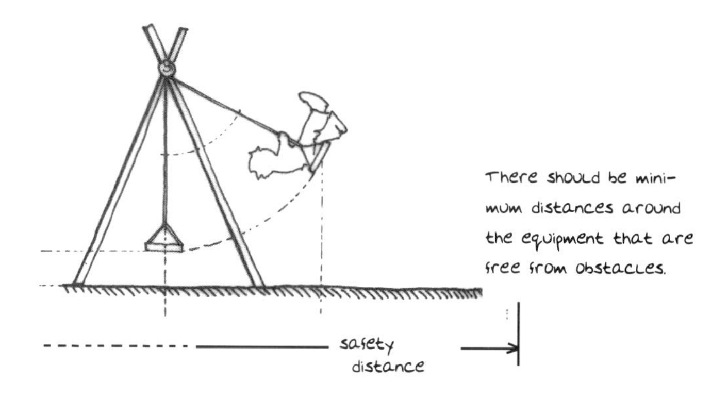

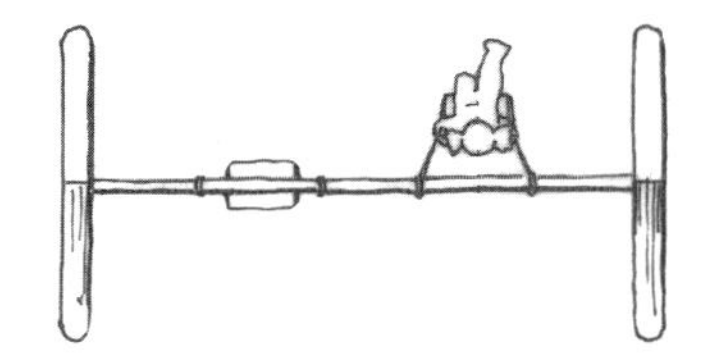

A surface that pads or absorbs impact should be placed beneath the seats. This surface might be synthetic or natural; non-compact materials are usually used. (For materials which pad impacts, see section 3.1)

2.4 Climbing

The activity of climbing is basic for developing a child's motor abilities; through climbing, a child learns body control, balance and coordination between arms and legs. Since climbing comes so naturally to children, elements that encourage safe climbing are recommended in a playground.
A basic installation for climbing might be made up of rigid elements, such as spatial structures or inclined surfaces with hand and foot supports. Flexible materials, such as ropes or cables, are commonly found in climbing structures. In any event, they enjoy an ample range of design possibilities and it is becoming increasingly common to see all manner of climbing structures in different playgrounds.

Climbing on rigid equipment

A simple sloped surface or low hill are elements that, by their very nature, inspire kids to climb. An easy way to equip them for this function is to incorporate supports or grips along the surface for hand and foot support. Naturally, these supports must comply with the requisites previously specified in section 3.1.

Hill structure for climbing

The classic "monkey bars" structure.

Among the available wooden or metal structures can be found the classic arch, the domed configuration of bars, or structures with horizontal ladders, bars, rings and combined elements.
Climbing posts, which children can also slide down, can be included in this category as well. The surface of these posts should be entirely free from all welding traces or discontinuities and the sliding section should be straight, that is: with no changes in direction.

Climbing on flexible equipment

Climbing on flexible elements requires greater skills of balance than with rigid structures. This makes it especially advisable to not include this type of equipment in play areas designed for very small children.
Ropes can be fastened at one or both ends. In the former case, the rope should be sufficiently rigid so as to avoid getting tangled. The weave of both simple ropes and nets should have a smooth, non-slip outer skin.
Stops or fastenings are recommended in the intersection of nets in order to keep the knots from sliding. Ropes that do not have intersections should be adequately tensed so as to eliminate any risk of strangulation.

Climbing ropes fastened at both ends.

Climbing nets can be made up of ropes or galvanized cables.

The recommended diameter for ropes fastened at one end ranges between 25 and 45 mm; the rest can be anywhere from 18 to 45 mm.
Braided metal cables can offer an alternative to ropes and nets. The cable should be covered with a sheath, preferably of natural fiber, although it can be synthetic. Cables should be galvanized and properly tensed so as not to buckle, unravel or knot up. These elements must be manufactured with corrosion-resistant materials.

2.5 Composite Playground Equipment

composite equipment multiplies the play options.

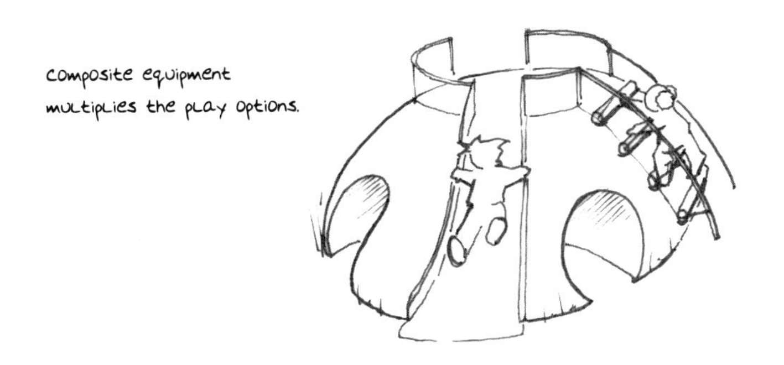

The trend in today's playgrounds is to incorporate equipment which has traditionally served a single function into more complex and versatile modular structures. Indeed, when a simple seesaw or slide becomes part of a combined structure, a whole new field of possible uses is opened.
Good playground equipment should be designed for easy modification and adaptation to the different needs of the children who will be using it. As far as possible, composite structures should be equipped to offer different degrees of difficulty.

2.6 Playing with Nothing - Shapes

The imagination itself is one of a child's most important and effective instruments; which is why a given piece of equipment may seem very simple to us, but highly elaborate in the eyes of a child. We may even find it incomprehensible how that piece can come to be the favorite, even in the presence of equipment which we find to be better thought out or designed.

Any shape can serve to stimulate the imagination.

Drawings and games in the sand.

Undefined, abstract elements, such as a mound of rocks or a pile of sand, are often much more fun or interesting for children than objects that represent something concrete or specific. This is why it is recommendable to avoid realistic designs -copies of real objects such as trains, cars and houses- in playground equipment. Suggestion over representation in a playground can be much more effective.
In creating "undefined" spaces with no specific intention, we encourage experimentation and creativity and provide the opportunity for multiple uses, as many as a child's imagination can conjure. Through these undefined spaces, children can create and develop their own references.

2.7 Learning through the Senses

Elements which stimulate the senses are especially recommended for children, particularly those who suffer some form of perceptual, psychological or sensorial impairment.
Installations equipped with specific elements that encourage listening, looking, touching and even smelling can be included. Children can actively participate and interact with acoustic, visual, tactile and olfactory phenomena while at the same time learning how their own actions elicit certain responses, whose effect they may or may not understand.
Equipment designed to stimulate the senses is being seen more and more in the design of new playgrounds. The idea is to improve upon the traditional concept that playground equipment should just be fun, now incorporating educational aspects and encouraging interaction among children.

Sounds

Children love to make sound by banging on objects or rubbing them together, which is probably why we find increasingly more playgrounds featuring sound-producing equipment. The options are numerous, whether we make use of natural elements or come up with a specific system, with the end result being generally appreciated by all age groups, including adults.

The breeze blowing through bamboo.

Percussion with tubes tuned to a musical scale.

Although sounds produced naturally, for example by a breeze gently blowing through plants or the leaves of a tree, are pleasing in their own right, children will especially enjoy elements with which they can interact and experiment. A good option is to incorporate percussion systems, whistles, xylophones, and more at different points of the playground; or perhaps concave spaces, tubular and parabolic objects - anything that generates echoes, amplifications, vibrations and other effects which are often as pleasing as they are instructive.

Playing with echoes.

Watch, see, observe

In the same way that we might incorporate acoustic games, we can also design elements that play with optical effects - elements such as magnifying glasses, reflective material, prisms, kaleidoscopes, overlapping elements or color transparencies.
We can come up with an endless variety of designs for a playground, taking as inspiration experiments found in a science museum, for example; such a design would fulfill the dual function of educating and entertaining.
We often relate the sense of sight with color perception. Although it is said that children respond better to primary colors, there does not seem to be any real basis for such a statement. What is certain is that children with impaired vision find guiding references in bright colors and well defined shapes. Keeping this in mind, we will choose bright colors to stimulate visual perception, especially in those areas designed for children with difficulties, while at the same time avoiding visually overloading the rest of the playground installations.

Tools for playing with optical effects are as fun as they are educational.

Touch and texture

Experimenting with textures

We have made brief mention of the usefulness of including texture changes in paving materials in order to guide children with visual impairments. The use of different textures can also provide information about a play area, a type of apparatus or a discontinuity in the surroundings. We can establish the difference between spaces and equipment by combining various surface finishes or we can use this resource simply as another play element, encouraging a sense of discovery among small children or those with little to no eyesight, and providing a contrast between soft and hard material, dense and fluid, dry and wet, smooth and rough.

...and smell!

We do not often view the sense of smell in the same way as the other senses; although smells and their many variations are an important guiding factor for the blind or individuals with impaired vision. It might be a good idea to border paths through the park with highly fragrant plants. This olfactory and spatial system will help users find their way around the different areas of the park.

Odors can also serve as spatial references.

2.8 Building - playing with sand and mud

Children in all times and all places have naturally enjoyed playing with sand and mud, which are perfect for digging, building, sculpting, filling and emptying buckets and mixing with water. The areas set aside for this type of activity should be calm places shielded from the wind, with plenty of sun as well as partially covered by shade. It is also a good idea to keep them separated from the areas where the bigger kids play, areas where a heightened level of activity is the norm. This physical separation can be a fence, wall or shrubbery, which also imparts the feel of a calm, cozy environment.

These areas should be shielded from the wind and should include both sunny and partially shady areas.

Since it is ordinarily the smallest children that most enjoy playing with sand and mud, we need to keep in mind that a supervising adult will be in attendance. Therefore, benches or some other form of seating should be included alongside these play areas.
Part of the sandbox can be adapted for playing with mud, in which case some sort of drainage system will have to be included in order to evacuate excess water. Sandy surfaces, we should remember, are not the most suitable for getting around in a wheelchair. Raised sandboxes might be a good solution for allowing all children to comfortably reach them. We can also include different types of sand, with varying thicknesses of grain, in order to provide an array of touch sensations and degrees of cohesion. The sand should be periodically removed, cleaned and renewed to keep it from hardening and to prevent minor injuries.

2.9 Splashing around - playing with water

Water offers a range of stimuli for children, from the sensations of wet and dry, to experimenting with submerged and floating objects, to changes in temperature, and so forth. Since water is a privileged feature seen only rarely in playgrounds, it might be a good idea to consider the possibility of bringing in water via artificial means - climate and resources permitting.

Learning about the properties of water.

Streams, canals, ponds, fountains and sprinklers can all be built, thereby gaining highly attractive, not to mention educational, play areas. Water consumption and evacuation in a "wet" play zone that enjoys its own source of water should be controllable.
For safety reasons, the water should be drinkable and it should be no deeper than 35 to 40 centimeters.

To decrease the risk of slips and falls, the borders of wet zones should be well defined and constructed with non-slip material. As with sandboxes, a space where adults can sit and supervise the water zone should be included.
We mustn't forget that even the sensation of water can be imparted more or less directly via bridges and raised walkways. So, with or without water, these elements can always be incorporated into the design of a playground. The imagination will provide the river!

2.10 On wheels

If sufficient space is available, areas for skating, bicycling or even tricycling (as long as safety is ensured) are a wonderful addition to a playground or park. Mid- to large-sized bicycles, skates and other apparatuses which can reach dangerous speeds may present a danger to other park visitors. Therefore, their use should be circumscribed to specific routes and should be independent of the rest of the park. These routes can run parallel to other primary paths or independent of them; and they should be well marked.
Additionally, bike racks should be included. If the park does not include bike paths, the area for locking up the bikes should be located near the park entrance so that they can be picked up when visitors to the park leave.

Bike paths should have
clearly defined
boundaries.

3 Ensuring Safe Play Conditions

When we define any easy-to-do activity as "child's play", chances are we are not thinking of what really goes on in a children's playground, where bumps and falls are the norm.
It's not difficult to imagine how the youngest children are the most susceptible to having the greatest number of falls and accidents; although bigger kids also play on equipment with varying levels of difficulty - equipment whose correct or incorrect usage might involve certain risks. While most of the falls caused by a loss of balance while playing are difficult to avoid, we can dampen those falls by installing shock-absorbent paving, which is anything ranging from sand to the increasingly popular variety of synthetic materials.
Other kinds of possible accidents that may occur in a playground are those caused by the use of the equipment itself - run-ins with fixed or moveable elements, or a child getting body parts or clothes stuck in the equipment, all of which can be very dangerous. Such accidents, however, can easily be avoided. There are a series of regulations guiding the dimensions to which play equipment should be built and the minimum distances between various parts, all according to the characteristics of each given piece.
Safety issues in areas with as much activity as in a playground are complex and subject to many factors. Following are concise descriptions of some of the design considerations to bear in mind when creating playground equipment from the standpoint of preventing accidents.

3.1 Padding Impact

The most frequent accidents caused by slipping are those where there is a patch of sand and gravel spread over a smooth surface. This can be avoided by ensuring that loose paving does not spread to nearby hard or continuous ground surfaces. Puddles can also cause slips, making it necessary to install a good system of rainwater evacuation as well as a non-slip paving material.

The ground surface beneath playground equipment should be impact absorbant.

Its thickness should be sufficient to attenuate falls.

minimum 30 cm

The areas prone to the greatest risk of falls are those that are below or around play equipment. The most frequently used impact-absorbent materials that are spread over such ground surfaces are tree bark, wood chips, sand and gravel.
A minimum depth of 30 cm with a good drainage system is recommended for the impact absorbing properties of the material to be as efficient as possible. Additionally, in order to ensure that they continue working, they should receive continuous upkeep and periodic renovation.

Be careful with loose paving: it can cause slips if it spills over onto continuous paving.

While grass can also pad falls very efficiently, its degree of efficacy varies greatly according to the effects of certain weather conditions and geographical locations. Furthermore, it is subject to growth cycles and very heavy wear and tear in circulation routes and areas where the impact is constant.

Grass suffers excessive wear and tear in frequently-used areas.

Synthetic paving creates uniform surfaces and comes in a variety of colors.

Synthetic materials such as rubber or recycled foam provide the basis for smooth, homogenous surfaces (making them easily accessible for persons with reduced mobility). They can be custom designed to absorb varying levels of impact; additionally, their range of color options enriches the design. Although these materials are generally more expensive, once installed they require a minimum amount of maintenance.

3.2 Minimum Space

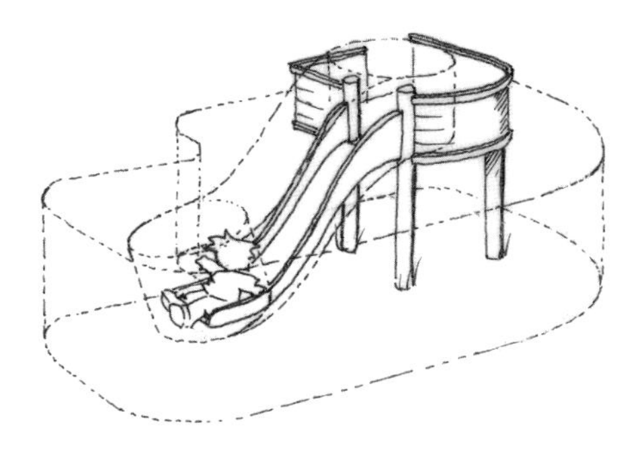

All play equipment requires some amount of space, however minimum, for its use. Such space comprises, logically, the volume occupied by the equipment itself, as well as a certain amount of the surrounding area that should be kept clear of obstacles so that the equipment may be safely and efficiently put to use.
The different regulations governing the use of playground equipment include calculations and tables for determining the safety margins necessary for each type of apparatus according to its properties and the use to which it will be put.

The area of impact

In order to minimize the risk of collisions between children, a safety zone should be created around any equipment whose use involves abrupt movements. European standards establish an obstacle-free zone, called the area of impact, of one and a half meters around the outer perimeter of a piece of raised equipment from which a child could fall.
The area of impact must remain free of obstacles up to the height of this raised point: this area is called the "fall space" and is defined as the space which might be occupied by a user in the event of falling from that height.

A slide's area of impact

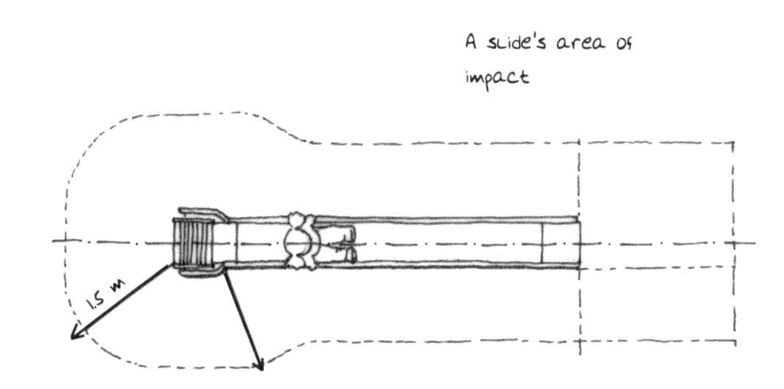

Obstacle-free fall height

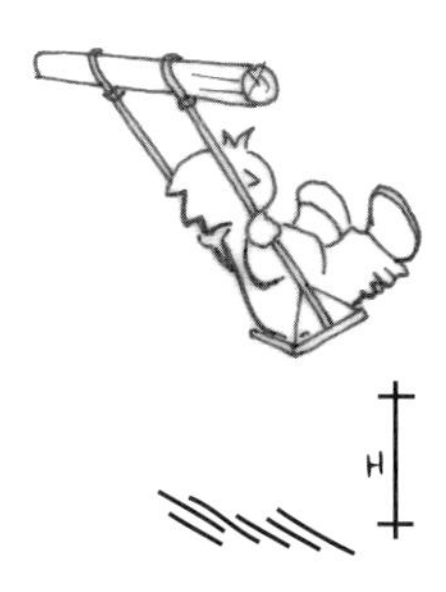

Fall height from a swing and from a platform.

The concept of the "obstacle-free fall height" is a determining factor when choosing the type of paving for the area beneath a piece of equipment. In equipment that is used while standing, the obstacle-free space will extend from the foot support to the lower surface. If the equipment is used while sitting, the space is that between the seat and the lower surface; in pieces from which the user hangs, from the hand support to the lower surface.
In order to determine the obstacle-free fall height we must consider the possible movement of the equipment as well as its users.
By defining such concepts as "area of impact" or "fall height" we can begin to form an idea of the necessary parameters for ensuring that a play area is safe and that the risk of accidents caused by the equipment is minimized.

3.3 Protection Against Getting Stuck

Another possible playground danger is that children may get a body part or a piece of clothing stuck in openings that are too small or narrow. Again, there are standardized regulations guiding the design and dimensional requisites for minimizing this risk.
In general, elements in which body parts or clothing might get stuck are those which feature a closed perimeter, such as tunnel slides,

Be careful with moveable parts.

open tubes and nets, as well as apparatuses with an open perimeter, amongst which are grooves, cracks and V-shaped openings.
Moveable parts on playground equipment are also liable to cause entrapment, specifically between the moving parts and the ground, which is why we must respect the minimum safety distances for the equipment as stipulated in the corresponding regulations.

Getting the head or neck stuck

The head can get stuck in openings that are intended to be entered head first as well as those where the child enters feet first. Closed perimeter openings, slits, sharp angles, flexible elements (ropes, chains, nets), openings in fences and railings can all cause entrapment of the head and neck, which is why it is crucial to ensure the appropriate dimensions when designing them.

It is crucial to ensure the suitable dimensions in the design of playground equipment.

Getting the extremities stuck

The ends of tubes should be closed.

Let's turn our attention to those openings in which fingers might get stuck while the rest of the body is in motion, a situation that can occur when a child is sliding or swinging.
Entrapment of fingers and hands can also be caused by the open ends of tubes or pipes. We should therefore make sure that they are sealed off and that the seal cannot be removed without the use of tools.
In the event that a child has one or more extremities trapped in a raised or inclined point, a possible fall in this position could cause very serious injuries. We should eliminate this risk by paying special attention to the dimensions of those rigid openings and closed perimeter openings on surfaces where children can run or climb, especially if they are raised or inclined.